Comparative Literary Theory
– An Overview –

Comparative Literary Theory
– An Overview –

Kapil Kapoor

PRINTWORLD
Publishers of Indian Traditions

Cataloging in Publication Data – DK
[Courtesy: D.K. Agencies (P) Ltd. <docinfo@dkagencies.com>]

Kapoor, Kapil.
Comparative literary theory : an overview/Kapil Kapoor.
p. cm.
Includes bibliographical references (p.) and index.
ISBN 9788124607206

1. Literature – Philosophy. 2. Literature – Aesthetics. 3. Poetics. 4. Sanskrit poetry – History and criticism. I. Title.

DDC 801 23

ISBN 13: 978-81-246-0720-6
First published in India in 2014

Printed and published by:
D.K. Printworld (P) Ltd.
Regd. Office : *'Vedaśrī'*, F-395, Sudarshan Park
(Metro Station: Ramesh Nagar)
New Delhi - 110 015
Phones : (011) 2545 3975; 2546 6019; *Fax* : (011) 2546 5926
e-mail : indology@dkprintworld.com
Web : www.dkprintworld.com

Preface

Comparative Literary Theory: An Essay[1]

ONLY two cultures have thought about literature – the classical Indian and Greek. The contemporary Western literary thinking is naturally sourced from the Greek thought, particularly of the three great minds – Socrates, Plato and Aristotle – that has proliferated into and finds expression in the literatures of modern European languages, inflected in the process by Latin as the expresser of Christian thought. The multilingual Indian tradition, sourced originally from the classical Tamil, Pali, Prakrit and Sanskrit, has evolved through known phases and proliferated into and finds expression in the literatures, both written and oral, of not only the modern Indian languages but also in the literatures of numerous small communities often patronizingly referred to as "tribal" literatures.

Cultural specificity marks these two traditions off from each other but the universal human condition that finds expression in all literatures binds them together. We hope to show it by describing and examining the subject in seven chapters:

1. Growth of Poetics as a Discipline
2. Theory of Literature
3. Categories of Literarv Artefacts
4. Aesthetics of Literature as an Art Form

[1] Written as UGC Emeritus Fellow at Jawaharlal Nehru University (JNU), New Delhi, 2007-09.

5. Philosophy of Literature
6. Characteristic Cultural Exprersions, Sublime and Śṛṅgāra.
7. Theorizing Theory.

Before we go on to analyse these aspects one by one, it is useful to distinguish literary theory/poetics and literary criticism. What both theory and criticism have to do with literature is in fact post-literature, i.e. follow and make sense of literary practices. In principle, it is possible to draw a line between the two – literary theory and literary criticism. Literary theory is concerned with general questions about literature: What are the properties common to all literatures? What is the function of literature? What different forms does literature take? What is the nature of literary creativity? What are the elements of form and meaning in different kinds of literary compositions? What is the nature of literary meaning? What is the relationship between a literary composition and (a) its author, (b) its readers, and (c) its age and context?

Literary criticism, on the other hand, is concerned with the merit of this or that literary composition, properties of actual concrete examples of literature, the individuality of a work, its style in the broadest sense, the choice of matter as well as technique and language. Literary criticism may take up any or all of the criteria of literary theory (listed in the preceding paragraph) with reference to concrete works of art.

But the two kinds of inquiry are not really independent of each other. Theory of literature cannot be discussed without reference to facts and artefacts of literature and particular literary works can be examined only in the perspective of the theoretical parameters of literature. Even if the word "criticism" is confined to assessment of merit of a work or interpretation of its meaning, there can be no validity in the exercise unless its analysis can appeal to general intellectual principles. Thus theory and criticism necessarily overlap. And this may account for certain indeterminacy in the use of the two terms. Literary criticism can and often does include a reference to literary theory, in such collocations as "theoretical literary criticism" as against "applied literary criticism". But the European way of keeping the two separate by referring to them as "poetics" and "literary criticism" is to be commended.

However, there is a difference of focus in the two traditions. While the Western tradition moved more and more in the direction of literary criticism, the Indian tradition of thought continued to focus on theoretical questions of literature and its elements. This may be due to the fact that the Indian tradition is far more homogeneous – its source is one, the Indian philosophy. At the roots of the Western tradition, on the other hand, there are three springs – Judaic, Greek and Christian – a fact that led to what may be judged, depending on how one reads it, as a kind of either amalgamation or dispersal of thought. So the discipline of poetics moves from "Pagan" Greek to Christian to what in modern times can interestingly be understood as "Judaic" in its application-impulse, "doing" as against "thinking" as Matthew Arnold had anticipated in his *Culture and Anarchy*.

Contents

1

Growth of Poetics as a Discipline

Rise and Formation of the Discipline of Poetics in the West[1]

THE West does not, come to think of it, actually have a "tradition" of literary thinking in the sense that there are breaks/"ruptures" and, therefore, often re-starts. After, the Greek thinkers, there is a break of about 300 years before Longinus picks up Aristotle again and explains his theory of literature in his essay "On the Sublime". Then there is another break of about 150 years before the Alexandrians talk of the greatness of Greek literature and the need to study it in translation. Another break and then the Roman rhetoricians make a practical study of the Greek masters, of their "rhetoric", their art of composition reinforcing the Alexandrian trend of "literary criticism" (as against literary theory). Another break before St. Augustine inflects "pagan" aesthetics with Christian idealism. Another 1,100 years before Thomas A. Kempis sets out to wed Christian thought with Platonic idealism, i.e. Platonism. The renaissance has taken place and the Greek masters are studied as models and the trend of literary criticism, the analysis of the Greek masters, gets strengthened. "Theorists" such as Sidney and Shelley are not original – they

---

[1] For the first statement of this, please see our book *Canonical Texts of English Literary Criticism with Selections from Classical Poeticians* (with Ranga Kapoor). New Delhi: Academic Foundation, 1995.

paraphrase the theory as it comes down from the Greeks and relate it, marginally, to their literature.

In the nineteenth-century Europe, particularly in Germany and France, with the widespread establishment of Sanskrit studies a new thought movement germinates and spreads, the movement that comes to be called German romanticism. It impacted literary theory as well, and thinkers such as Schiller, Schopenhauer and Nietzsche dwelt on general questions of literature. It impacted more strongly the study of language with Sanskritists such as Saussure, Trubetzkoy and Roman Jakobson breaking new ground in descriptive linguistics that resulted in the formulation of structuralism – a new way of looking at language and its relationship to the world. It is a thought movement that has shaped the entire modern Western thought from structuralism to post-modernism. Contemporary "theory" is a product of this thinking and therefore has understandable affinities with Indian structural literary theories.

Thinking about literature must be as old as literature itself. In the West, the attested beginnings of "poetics", the science (or study) of literature, are located in ancient Greece, in the many reflections about poetry and poets in the dialogues of Plato. The first formal text of literary theory in that tradition is of course the justly celebrated *Poetics* of Aristotle.

Plato had asked and answered some fundamental questions about the nature of reality, the nature and status of representations of reality in art, the nature and source of artistic creativity and the status of literature as a verbal discourse and its status as a discourse of knowledge in relation to the other rational discourses, for example, of philosophy and history. Aristotle, as an able disciple of Plato, built further on these foundations and developed a general theory of literature (with reference to the tragic and the epic poetry) which differed in significant ways from Plato's enunciations. For

Aristotle, literature is a more valid epistemology than either philosophy or history – Homer's Truth, in his argument, is more abstract and therefore more universal than that of Herodotus or Socrates. In his theorizing about "plausible lies", Aristotle establishes a distinction between the reality of life and the reality of art, and in his analyses of "means", "objects" and "manner" of imitations, he assumes and implies that all art, including literature, is as much a product of "craft" as of inspiration. Aristotle's *Poetics* is a seminal text in the Western tradition. Its historical importance is undeniable – all subsequent works in literary theory are either an extension or a reinterpretation of Aristotle. It is only when we reach the late nineteenth century,[2] that we find different literary concerns – a foregrounded concern with the linguistic materiality of literature and with meaning as a linguistic construct, though this too is not in complete disjunction with the classical theory.

Aristotle was followed by Horace whose *Ars Poetica* (*Art of Poetry*), around 65-8 BCE, is a kind of "edited restatement" of Aristotle's *Poetics* in the sense that Horace takes up a few major issues in his own order of treatment and restates Aristotle's position on those issues in his own language (and in verse). The focus is of course "contemporary" as Horace has the Roman practitioners of poetry and criticism in his mind as his audience. If one were to search for one single principle

---

2 The shift in the paradigm takes place as a result of Europe's active engagement and interaction with Sanskrit thought. Sanskrit chairs had been established in all premier European universities by 1810, and almost all the major nineteenth-century European scholars – Schopenhauer, Hegel, Nietzsche, Kant, Schiller, Schelling, de Saussure – were either Sanskritists or, on their own testimony, influenced by Sanskrit theories and models. Sanskrit thought made possible the structuralist revolution in the social and natural sciences and de Saussure's "phonocentric revolution" generated new modes of literary thinking later evident in twentieth-century theories.

upheld by Horace, it must be "fidelity", an Aristotelian imperative of not wandering too far away from things as they actually are. Horace is followed by Longinus. Longinus' essay "On the Sublime" does not directly echo Aristotle nor does it seem to be directly related to Horace – but the linkages are there. Aristotle's discussions in *Poetics*, of what the poet is to aim at and what he is to avoid and what are the conditions on which the tragic effect depends (section 13), of the sources of fear and pity (section 14), of the importance of moral purpose (section 15), of the form of discovery (section 16) and Aristotle's analysis of diction particularly of the role of metaphor (section 22), are clearly the original impulses for Longinus' discussion of the sublime subject and sublime expression. Aristotle and Longinus are bridged by Horace's discussion of diction and by Demetrius' *On Style in Poetics* . . . who divides literary expression into "plain", "stately", "polished" and "powerful". Longinus' principle of "sublimity", apart from being a descriptive category, is also an evaluative measure that can explain why "some works please all men at all times". Longinus comes at the end of almost two centuries of painstaking scholarship of the School of Alexandria and the beginning of what may be termed as the Roman School or Rhetoric.

Between the decline of Athens (of Greece) and this Roman phase, the two centres of learning were Pergamon and Alexandria, both in North Africa, and both referred to as the School of Alexandria. No work of poetics of this prolific period of two centuries is available now and whatever we know is reconstructed from references in other works. We know that this age was remarkable for its scholarship made possible by the massive Alexandrian library. We also know that for more than a century Homer was the object of study – Zenodotus (325–234 BCE) prepared an authentic edition of Homer and Aristarchus ". . . the first 'critic' in antiquity . . . earned his name by a programme of studying Homer in the light of the Homeric age, dialect, and idiom" (Wimsatt and Brooks 1957: 78). Two issues of theoretical importance that get foregrounded in the work of this period are the opposition between history and criticism, and the relative merits of ancients and moderns.

A concern with language, a recognition of the excellence of the Greek masters and a painful awareness of the decline of literature in the contemporary (modern) times – these were the three features of the literary activity at the School of Alexandria and these were the three concerns of Longinus as well. In his grasp of the rhetoric of literary discourse, the diction, the syntax and the figures of speech, and in his great stress on language as an equally important, if not the primary, constituent of the sublime, Longinus both *anticipates* and *is* a Roman. That Longinus' concerns and values continued to be the concerns and values of the Roman critics is evident when we review the works of Dio of Prusa, Tacitus and Plutarch. In what may be called the late classical age, many, including the Greek rhetoricians, worked in the time of the Roman empire. There was not much contemporary literature worthy of note and the classical Greek literature was being translated and adapted for the Roman audience. The later classical critics bemoan the decline of literature and analyse the Greek masters to demonstrate the excellence that was responsible for the survival and popularity of the Greek masters in another time and at another place. This was Longinus' concept of the "sublime", or the quality that makes a work stand the test of time. The later classical critics take off from this to explicate what elements constitute the sublime in earlier literature and how to account for decadence in their own age. They suggest that a study of the masters, an understanding of what constitutes great literature, is one way of renewing contemporary literature.

Dio Chrysostomus was the most eminent of the Greek rhetoricians and sophists, born at Prusa in Bithynia about the middle of the first century CE. In his essay "Philoctetes in the Tragedians" (Oration 52) he argues that simplicity of form is the mark of great literature and the substance of "sublimity" is what makes a work survive. Dio makes a comparative analysis of three tragedies written by Aeschylus, Euripides and Sophocles on the same theme of Odysseus's theft of Philoctetes' bow. From the differences of treatment of the same theme, he builds up a theory of "greatness" in art. Aeschylus has "grandeur and archaic splendour" and "this is altogether simpler and more tragic, in contrast with Euripides' more sophisticated and painstaking treatment". Aeschylus is often not realistic, but then "poets often represent heralds as making several days' journey in one day". Thus while subscribing on the one hand to the Aristotelian demand of "perspicuity", he does allow the violation of the Aristotelian notion of "order" and "unity" in a tragedy. Comparing Euripides, he notes the moral content of Euripides' art, "the lyrics afford not only pleasure but many exhortations to virtue" as well. He always has a message but that does not make Euripides a better tragedian. In opposition to the Platonic requirement of truth and value in literature, Dio relegates "virtue" and considers both Aeschylus and Sophocles greater than Euripides, Aeschylus being the greatest on account of his simplicity and grandeur:

> Sophocles comes between the two. He possesses neither Aeschylus' originality and simplicity, nor the craftsmanship, shrewdness, and rhetorical effectiveness of Euripides. . . . At the same time, his management of the story is excellent and convincing.

The greatness of Sophocles is the greatness of his verse:

> His verse is dignified and grand, tragic and euphonious . . . combining great charm with sublimity and dignity.

Dio is a practising critic and a comparativist, and therefore a pioneer in the Western tradition. He does not blindly subscribe to the classical theory of literature as laid down by Plato and Aristotle. He boldly differs from both in the notions of "virtue" and "truth", respectively. Finally, he has a great regard for the Greek masters, a habit of mind that endures in the tradition. Contemporary literature, by implication, is not worthy of note.

On the last point, Tacitus, the next available rhetorician, is more explicit. Tacitus, born a little before CE 60, and a Roman, in his "Dialogue on Orators" asserts that . . .

> whole earlier periods were brightened by the lustre and talent of so many outstanding orators; our own tunes . . . find themselves barren.

He composes a Platonic dialogue with a number of speakers debating one subject after another in interrelated moves. The dialogue first debates the value of poetry and it is concluded that oratory is better than poetry – it brings more material benefit and more fame than poetry. This itself is an evidence of decadence – it is an age that finds no value for poetry: ". . . as for poems and verses. . . . They win their authors no respectable position and bring them no advantages. . . ." This dismissal of poetry is not to be related to Plato. Plato's objection to poetry is on moral grounds; the Roman objection is on material grounds, on grounds of utility for poetry brings no material success or benefits. The next speaker, Maternus, conducts the first attested defence of poetry. Maternus argues Homer is more famous than Demosthenes, Sophocles than Lysias and Virgil than Cicero. As for the material rewards, the poets are contented with their own simple lives and are against "profiteering":

> I don't want the escorts and ceremonious departures and crowds of callers. . . . I count it among the principal rewards of poetry that it is composed away from the bustle and . . .

> the mind is free to withdraw to fresh innocent places, and enjoy a holy world.

And because they are "freemen", the poets actually enjoy a higher status. At this point, another speaker joins the debate to say that even in oratory, the ancient masters were much greater than the contemporary ones. It is contended that style changes with times and that the more ornate style of Rome is needed by the faster Roman age. This view is contradicted and it is argued that ornamentation is a mark of decadence when judged against "the ancient habit of plain speaking".

Attempt is then made to account for this decadence. It is suggested that strong centralized rule (imperialism) and stability produce stagnation in the arts. Democracy, with its lack of strict order, is more conducive to creativity:

> The great and famous eloquence I have in mind is the nurseling of licence – which fools call liberty – and the companion of sedition: it unbridles and spurs on the people; it has no respect for persons, no proper dignity; it is insolent, rash, arrogant; in well-organized states it does not arise.

It is asserted at the end that no age can have both great fame and great peace, and the tone of the text suggests that "fame" is better than peace. To recover from the decadence of its times, this text too, like that of Dio, looks back on and up to the "ancients" and sees hope in their simplicity and sublimity. Identifying individual liberty as the condition of excellence in creative arts Tacitus goes beyond Dio.

The third critic of note is Plutarch, a Greek biographer and philosopher. The work which has immortalized him is his *Parallel Lives of Greeks and Romans* (sixteenth-century English version by North). His other writings, above sixty in number, are placed under the general title of *Moralia* or ethical works. Plutarch's *On the Study of Poetry*, after Plato's reflections and Aristotle's observations, is the first available examination of the nature of poetry. Plutarch is discussing how to read poetry rightly. To prevent the ill effects of "the deceitfulness of poetry" on the young minds, Plutarch does not like Plato banish poets and poetry, instead he advocates a tempering of poetry with philosophy.

Poetry is full of voluntary and involuntary lies: voluntary lies are the deliberate constructs of the poet, while involuntary lies are the poet's actual misconceptions. The reader who accepts these two kinds of statements as true:

> . . . is lost, and his judgement ruined. The reader who remembers and clearly bears in mind the magic of fiction that poetry possesses . . . will come to no harm. . . .

To be able to perceive fictions, the reader has to be well-versed in philosophy and remember "the fact that poetry is not concerned with truth". This notion of poetry as untrue is only apparently Platonic, for the departure in Plutarch lies in his requirement of a philosophical and moralist reading of poetry rather than a total rejection of poetry. He believes like Plato that every poem is an act of imitation; however, unlike Plato he asserts that the reader is aware of this fact and therefore, never seeks truth or beauty in poetry – he appreciates and admires the quality of imitation:

> . . . poetry is an art of imitation, a capacity analogous to painting . . . we feel pleasure and admiration not because it is beautiful but because it is like.

When the poet portrays evil, it is for verisimilitude and one must not assume that the poet endorses that evil:

> poets simply attribute vile and shocking words to vile and shocking characters . . .

Life has both good and evil, and poetry being an imitation of life, naturally has both the elements. The reader therefore must read attentively and comprehensively in order to evaluate the poet's statements:

> . . . Poetry, he must realize, is an imitation of the manners' and lives of men, who are not perfect, pure and irreproachable, but involved in passions, false opinions and ignorance. . . .

He advocates critical reading:

> . . . we must accustom ourselves to commenting with confidence, and saying "wrong" and "inappropriate" as often as we say "right" and "appropriate".

Plutarch says, we may, if need be, evaluate the ideas of a poet and compare him with other poets. Thus Plutarch advocates "close, critical, comparative" study of poetry.

These three texts react against the decadence of their age and to shed its decadence revert to the heritage of Greek literature to set the Greeks as models to be followed for literature. Dio foregrounds "simplicity" and "sublimity" as values of literature; Tacitus stresses individual "liberty" and democracy as conditions of great literature and Plutarch codes a proper "reading strategy" to get the best out of poetry (literature). Dio addressed the contemporary poets, Tacitus had the contemporary statesmen and Plutarch the readers in mind.

The goal of this later classical criticism is quite clear – to assist at a renaissance of Roman literature by inferring from the Greek masters a theory of what constitutes great literature. The Roman phase matured into the Age of Rhetoric and continued the later classical preoccupation with language and style of literature. The place of oratory in Roman socio-political life explains this focus on rhetoric. Aristotle's work by that name came to be studied closely and the literary language also came to be studied chiefly for its rhetorical values. This explains the elaboration and systematization of figures of speech and also Longinus' prolonged discussion of the linguistic and rhetorical elements of the language of literature.

The middle ages continued this Roman interest in rhetoric. But there is another important strand in medieval thought which has strong bearings on literary theory – the philosophical reflections on the nature of reality which develop into a theory of what constitutes beauty and into a theory of aesthetics. We shall only touch upon this tradition of thought, the Neo-Platonism that binds Plotinus (CE 205-70), St. Augustine (CE 354–430) and Thomas Aquinas (CE 1225-74). These three are essentially theologians, Christian theologians, who are examining the relationship between this visible universe and the Divine. Divinity, according to Plotinus, who wrote his *Enneads* in Greek, includes all beings and constitutes the unity of all beings. The material universe is fragmented, multiple and without order or form. It is the idea, the divinity that organizes this reality into form and being. "Order" or pattern imposed by the ideal form constitutes beauty and it is this beauty that gives pleasure, ". . . the principle of order observed in visible things . . . this vast orderliness". The artists when they reproduces objects, "give no bare reproduction . . . but go back to the ideas . . . they are moulders of beauty *and add where nature is lacking* (italics ours)." This of course is close to Aristotle's theory of objects . . . *as they ought to be* (*Poetics* 2S), and also is an expansion of Plato's theory of images, of "appearing" or "seeming" without really "being" (Sophist). This is "ordering" of parts of a complex object – achievement of a "symmetry" and where there are no parts to an object, where we have a substance, say "water or gold", the principle of "symmetry" does not apply – instead we have the "brightness" principle. Whatever is "bright" pleases the viewer and whatever pleases the viewer is beautiful. This "brightness" may in fact also be a "symmetry" of highly subtle, minute internal *differentia*. Both "symmetry" and "brightness" are based in the senses of sight and hearing, but sight comes first – "beauty addresses itself chiefly to sight".

Where does this "beauty" reside? Is it inherent in the object? Plotinus says no – the beauty is conferred by craftsmanship, by the craftsman – it is not in the material; it is in the designer – before it enters stone.

The idea that "beauty", that is "order" and "symmetry", is what the artist perceives in and imposes on a seemingly chaotic reality influenced St. Augustine, the Bishop of Hippo (North Africa), a Christian theologian and mystic philosopher. Neo-Platonism enabled St. Augustine, a prominent patristic, to pursue the Christian theological imperative of adapting the pagan philosophy of Hellenism to Christianity. Beauty, thus, a pagan principle, is seen to consist in the "unity" of an object, its totality and integrity and "unity" is the determining feature of all being and the source of all being is one divinity. A continuity between an abstract Divine Being and the multiple material reality is thus achieved. Objects are beautiful by virtue of their perfection (in terms of unity) and this "perfection" exists in the apparent imperfection, the "order" exists in the apparent chaos. Our human minds are endowed with an innate ability to cognize this perfection. The artist, more than the ordinary human beings, is tuned to perceive order in chaos, beauty in ugliness. In fact, as "order" can be cognized only in the presence of chaos, harmony in the presence of discord, and beauty in ugliness, the artist creates a world which is full of disorder, chaos and ugliness, and which yet manifests a transcendental order, unity and beauty. The artist's world, in this sense, is an analogue of the universe created by the Divine. These and such other aesthetic notions anticipate the concept of closure or psychological reconstruction of complete forms found in modern Gestalt psychology and in general aesthetics according to which an artist as well as the viewer, while looking at an object, make sense of it in terms of an ideal that they have in their mind and which they impose on the particular object.

Nine hundred years later Thomas Aquinas changed the focus of Christian metaphysics from the Platonic ideal forms to an Aristotelian world of actually experienced natural substances, but this world, in Aquinas, is hierarchically arranged and points upwards: in an ascending order to a transcendental and personal God. The Platonic continuity is replaced by a clear distinction between God and the material world created by him, but in the realm of aesthetics, no fresh ground is broken. Beauty in Aquinas still has a subjective content – beautiful is what gives pleasure to the viewer. This also implies that the object relates harmoniously to the subject – the object is suitably comprehensible for the viewer/subject. It is this union of the subject and the object that makes the cognition of beauty and the consequent pleasure possible. The object itself has three properties: integrity, proportion and clarity – the parts constitute a recognizable whole (the object), the object (image) has a definable relationship with what it represents, and it has brightness or colour that makes it attractive. It is easy to see the pertinence of these aesthetic notions for literary compositions – need for form, need for symbolic or realistic representation and need for aesthetic values in the modes of representation. Apprehension of beauty is an act of disinterested contemplation, and the aesthetic pleasure in the contemplation of beauty (or reading a good poem) is different from other kinds of worldly pleasures, in being more enduring and more transforming (the way Wordsworth records the effect of the sight of daffodils in his *Daffodils*). Beauty is relative and predicated for each object separately as it belongs to objects, and therefore all objects are more or less beautiful. Art, therefore, is nothing but right representation. In the Middle Ages of Europe, therefore, art was simply the right way of doing things and no distinction was made between making a cowshed and a cathedral, or between pottery and poetry.

It is right for us to remind ourselves that these aesthetic theories of the Middle Ages have proved remarkably enduring. After a brief sceptical, scientific interregnum in the fifteenth and sixteenth centuries, there was a revival of idealistic thought in the late seventeenth century in Germany, a flowering of this thought in the eighteenth century so that by the end of nineteenth century, many forms of idealism flourished – romantic, neo-platonic, symbolic, expressionist. Strands of German idealism travelled to England through the writings of Coleridge and Carlyle and were the governing aesthetics of the nineteenth century and James Joyce a high priest of this neothomist aesthetics with its creed of integrity, proportion and clarity in his *Stephen Hero* (1944: 213), in the twentieth century.

Apart from rhetoricians and theologians, medieval schoolmen were also concerned with some aspects of literary criticism. In grammar, metre and poetic meaning were studied. Metrical thinking became important with the rise of the vernacular literatures, when there came about a change from quantitative, non-accentual verse to accentual poetry. This involved a study of spoken languages and of the relationship between the rhythms of speech and the rhythms of poetry. The letters of Bishop Appolinario and *Ars Metrica* of venerable Bede are mentioned in this connection. In the interpretation of secular poetry, the schoolmen adapted some of the methods church exegetes had developed to interpret the scriptures. Thus study of verbal meanings became a major pedagogical concern and several kinds of meanings were identified – literal, historical, poetic (figurative), allegorical and symbolic. Both metre and meaning brought into focus the vernacular languages and literatures and this represents a major new interest for, till then literary theory and criticism were almost exclusively concerned with classical literatures. In this context, Dante (1265–1321) is a major landmark as he was the first to argue for the need to write in the vernaculars (*of the vulgar tongue* or *of writing in the vernaculars*).

The rise of vernacular literatures in the late Middle Ages coincided with the beginnings of the renaissance. Such widespread literary creativity invited study and analysis, and we notice a renewal and expansion of interest in classical literary theory and criticism. This new emphasis was first noticed in Italy from where it travelled all over Europe and England. The first evidence of this renewed interest is the revival of Aristotle's *Poetics*. It may be noted that Aristotle's work remained unknown throughout the Middle Ages. There was thus a break, a disjunction in the tradition of literary thought. The linkages were re-established with the first critical edition of *Poetics* in 1548 and, more importantly, with the first Italian translation in 1549. At the same time critical editions of all the major classical authors – Homer, Plato, Virgil, Horace – were also produced. This "helped to bring on a renaissance of furious theoretical activity an era of criticism. . .".

What were the important preoccupations of early renaissance? These were: (1) textual scholarship, (2) translation of classical texts into vernaculars, (3) explanation of classical theories and, most important of all, (4) the defence of vernacular languages, styles and literary forms and practices. It is at this point that we have the first text of English literary criticism – Sidney's *Defence of Poesie* (1595). Sidney carried into English thought the concerns and tasks of European literary criticism with this work. We have a continuous English tradition of critical texts and thinkers from Sidney onwards.

In England the discipline was frowned upon in the early phase. Rymer writing in 1674 says that "England is as empty of critics as of wolves", but the respectability of literary criticism as a worthy academic pursuit had been firmly established by Francis Bacon who in his *The Advancement of Learning* (1605) talked of the two traditions – critical and pedantic. He then went on to explain the critical function:

1. true correction and edition of authors
2. exposition and explication of authors
3. concerning the times to give true interpretation
4. concerning some brief censure and judgement of authors
5. concerning the syntax and disposition of studies.

Dryden was the first author to use the word "criticism" in its new sense of "evaluation". Writing in *The State of Innocence* (1677), he says:

> . . . by criticism as it was first instituted by Aristotle, was meant a standard of judging well.

Lord Kames (Henry Home) in 1762 ambitiously founded "the science of criticism". Criticism becomes an autonomous field of inquiry in opposition to creativity with Matthew Arnold and its domain is now wider than literature – it is the key to modern culture, a substitute of religion and an instrument of renewal and survival of societies. With J.C. Ransom (1941) the claims of criticism expanded even further to make it something like a total world-view or even a system of philosophy in a world that is more and more governed by the political imperatives. Thus poetics is once again enslaved to a larger discourse – the political. In the middle ages it was a part of rhetoric; in the eighteenth century it became a subdivision of philosophical aesthetics; with twentieth century, some of its important articulations, the Marxist and the sociological, became a part of the political discourse.

Twentieth century, however, marked the advent of poetics as an autonomous theoretical discipline. This is marked by a remarkable diversification and specialization of theoretical approaches. The twentieth-century literary theories, inspired by the structuralist revolution in linguistics, are all more or less centred in language in their goals and methods. *Russian Formalism* (1913-30) insists on the autonomy of literature, its independence from the author's biography, contemporary society and philosophical or religious theories. It is the literariness of literature that is investigated – hence Russian formalists researched in narrative structures, stylistic structures, and rhythmic and sound patterns. It is not the content but the modes or devices of expression that are the object of study of literature and how it relates to society through its patterns and structures which are perceived as social, and not individual, realities. The Morphological School of Germany rejected historicism and focused on literary forms and genres rather than the writer or his style. They investigated elementary forms like "enigma", "proverb" and "legend" and the registers of "speech" and "narrative composition". The verbal matter of the text remained their primary concern in all these investigations. New criticism also assumed a total autonomy of the text and investigated the constitution and the functioning of meaning – which is independent of the author and age – in literary texts. For the new critics, the poetic image is to be construed in terms of linguistic categories such as ambiguity, irony and paradox. Under the double influence of linguistics and ethnology, various structural analyses explored abstract patterns of form and meaning and narrative or textual structuralism. It is the "signifier" that is more important than the "signified" – the conditions of meaning rather than the meaning itself, the norm or system behind the variable features of discourse. Meaning is not a product of the author or of society but of the conventions of signs.

Various succeeding theories developed around structuralist methods of analysis – semiotics, psycho-analysis, de-construction, feminist theory. Some of these, for example the feminist theory, are later articulations of the Marxist theory which along with other sociological theories, did not consider literature as an autonomous series – rather, literature as a production like other social productions and amenable to the same producer – produce–consumer model of analysis. Influenced by Marx's philosophy of history, in this theory, "ideology" becomes a keyword and articulation, suppression or expansion of ideology becomes the function of literature. Psycho-analysis is yet another important modern approach influenced by the nineteenth-century researches in the workings of the human mind, particularly the work of Freud, Jung and Adler. It initially looked at literary meaning as an expression of the author's unconscious self and then as an interplay between the author's and the reader's minds. Under the influence of structuralism, now in the work of Lacan, it is the relationship between the language and the unconscious that is the object of study, how language structures and expresses desire.

Feminist readings of literature have gained popularity of late. Influenced by Marxism (and other sociological philosophies) and psycho-analysis, feminist poetics is the poetics of the underprivileged, the exploited and the marginalized. Beginning with a straightforward concern with women and themes related to women, it has now become an examination of how marginalization, exploitation and de-centring as crucial motivating drives are built, almost unconsciously, into language and other systems of cultural and artistic expression. In fact, poetic theories have been classified into four groups by M.H. Abrams on the basis of the four constitutive elements of the literary process – author, reader, work and universe. Theories differ in which of these elements is considered central. "Expressive theories" consider the author as the source and centre of a text and all literary meaning is the author's, the creator's intended meaning. "Pragmatic theories" consider the reader as the primary element in the literary process and all literary meaning is the reader's construct. "Objective theories" consider a literary work autonomous – independent of the author and the society – and literary meaning accordingly is abstract and a linguistic construct, that is constituted inside the text by the language itself. "Mimetic theories" consider a literary work as a reflection or representation of life and times and the meaning in literature is a social and contextual meaning. We can show that some major modern schools of criticism are based in one or the other poetic theory.

Expressive:	Psycho-analysis and the earlier romanticist theories (of Wordsworth and Coleridge).
Pragmatic:	Reception theory and reader-response theory
Objective:	Russian formalism, new criticism, structuralism (in all its realizations), morphological school.
Mimetic:	Marxist, sociological criticism, moral criticism.

There has been, evidently, considerable elaboration of the code of criticism in the twentieth century. The richness of the code has facilitated the acceptance of criticism as an academic discipline in the universities the world over. It is said that departments of literature now are teaching more criticism and less literature. In fact, contemporary criticism in the hands of thinkers like Barthes and Derrida has taken the form of meditative open-ended speculation, an auto-telic commentary which is as much about "itself" as about the literary object it is supposed to be commenting on. The contemporary critical commentary has challenged the familiar dichotomies of reading versus writing and primary versus secondary materials. The distinction between text and commentary was in any case not so clear in philosophy

– in literature, too, it has become indistinct. The "creative" and the "critical" so neatly opposed by Arnold (in *The Function of Criticism at the Present Time,* 1864) have now fused into a new philosophical criticism. Creative criticism, i.e. critical writing that has all the merits of a creative work, was in any case accepted by the poet-critics of the English tradition – Sidney, Dryden, Arnold, Coleridge, Eliot. When a kind of allegorical exegesis crosses over into the domain of literature not many eyebrows are likely to be raised. What we encounter in some contemporary critics is a new kind of writing – an essay that integrates literature, philosophy and criticism.

Contemporary "theory" emerged in the 1960s and marked a break from what is called the post-renaissance "humanist" tradition. "Theory", as it is known, has two cardinal roots – "relativity" and "linguistic constructivism" – one inspired by physics, quantum mechanics with its "uncertainty" principle in particular, and the other by linguistics with its Saussurean instability and consequential non-absoluteness of the linguistic sign in particular. All the fixities and certainties of the humanist tradition disappeared under this twin onslaught and the "singleness" of thought splintered into "many-ness" of all formulations about reality, life and literature. There are now n-number of "approaches" with one thing in common – all have language as their epistemology, i.e. for all schools of "theory", language is the evidence.

Rise and Formation of the Discipline of Poetics in India[3]

The rise and formation of the discipline of poetics in India has a different kind of history and concerns – it is a cogent history, continuous and cumulative, and the concerns or questions

[3] For the first statement of this theme see our book *Literary Theory: Indian Conceptual Framework* (in collaboration with Nalini M. Ratnam). New Delhi: Affiliated East-West Press, 1998.

addressed are typically characteristic of poetics. In the Western tradition, theory easily moves into what may is called "literary criticism". India's literary thinking consistently addresses questions of theory alone. For deep reasons, critical appraisal or evaluation of specific literary texts is virtually absent in Indian tradition of literary thought.

Kāvya-vidyā (poetics) has passed through well-defined stages. There is a reference to the first exposition (*upadeśa*) of this system. It was expounded by Lord Śiva – to his sixty-four disciples, which means first that this discipline has a beginning – it is not *anādi* – and it has an originator, though it is not possible to say who the originator was (as against the systems of philosophy which are associated with definite individuals, e.g. Kapila of Sāṁkhya, Jaimini of Mīmāṁsā) and, second, sixty-four "disciples" is to be interpreted to mean that on account of that exposition, sixty-four *kalās*[4] (arts and crafts) germinated, including song, dance, music, painting, calligraphy, cooking, garland making, ornaments making, knitting, printing, puppetry, magic, needlework, recitation, carpentry, etc. This gives a very broad definition to *kāvya-vidyā* – it is understood to mean a system of making, of representation and of arrangement.

So *kāvya-vidyā* is *upajñātā* (see Chapter 2). In the second stage, the *vidyā* is imparted by one of the sixty-four disciples, Brahmā himself, to *ṛṣis*, a term used for thinkers who among other things composed Sūtra texts. Therefore, in the second stage, thinkers and scholars begin to study *kāvya-vidyā* which in their hands becomes a system. There is another purpose here – the need to propagate the system to ensure welfare of the people. Thus, it is recognized as a useful discipline that

4 *Kalā* is defined as something that even a deaf or a dumb person can do (in Śukrācārya's *Nītisāra* 4.3). There are different enumerations of these sixty-four arts and crafts in, besides Śukrācārya, Vātsyāyana's *Kāmasūtra, Śrīmadbhāgavata,* Śrībāsavarājendra's *Svatattvaratnākara.*

promotes the welfare of people that could provide the motivation for systematizing the ideas pertaining to a branch of learning.

In the third stage, the stage of formalization, we have a comprehensive analysis and exposition of the discipline. We are told it was divided into eighteen topics – which represent an analysis of the subject – and it was expounded to those mature scholars who had undertaken and completed their education in *kāvya-vidyā* (*kāvya-vidyā snātakebhyad*). Thus systematized, it becomes a formal part of education (*śikṣā*) (acquiring *vidyā*).

In the fourth stage, we are told eighteen separate texts (*grantha* = that which is composed just as a garland is made) came to be composed, one on each of the eighteen divisions. Ostensibly, each text and division became in the course of time a specialization. Fifteen subjects or divisions are listed by Rājaśekhara. In this enumeration, there is:

1. an overlapping of areas (e.g. *ukti*, statement or utterance, and *svabhāvokti*, normal/natural utterance – a subdivision of *ukti* – are listed as separate subjects), and
2. a want of proper analysis of the subject matter, e.g. five of the fifteen subjects concern one figure of speech each.

So, it appears, this is a stage of proliferation – the discipline proliferates and loses clear definition and scope. If we review the primary texts of literary theory from Bhāmaha to Ānandavardhana, we find that each text has a different definition of literariness and has different focus – it is figures of speech or lexical mode or *rasa* or *guṇa/doṣa* or *dhvani* or language of literature and typology of literary forms. When information and ideas accumulate like this, there is need for a new systematization and that is identified as the stage of authentic statement.

In this fifth stage, an authentic Śāstra is prepared. Bharata's *Nāṭyaśāstra* is such a text for the theory of drama, comprehensive and authoritative. Is there such a text in *kāvya-vidyā*? The answer seems to be no though several primary texts for different aspects of literary theory have been in existence. Rājaśekhara suggests that his work composed in the style of a philosophy text (*darśana*, specifically Mīmāṁsā) is such a Śāstra. The claim cannot be evaluated because only a small part of the work has survived. But on the basis of the portion available – in itself very useful – it can be said that it is not like the Śāstra texts: it is explanatory in mode and includes examples and illustrations. Its language is not sūtraic (abbreviated). This method is typical of commentary texts. So, Rājaśekhara's *Kāvyamīmāṁsā* as also Mammaṭa's *Kāvyaprakāśa* are more like modern textbooks than Śāstras. The following topics are examined in the former:

1. scope of the Śāstra (discipline)
2. status and place of the discipline
3. origin of *kāvya*
4. morphological constructions and sentences
5. authentic text
6. meaning
7. proposition types
8. poet/composer
9. life and equipment of a poet/composer
10. relationship to society
11. intonation and meaning
12. echoes of other texts – in words and meaning
13. poetic convention
14. statements and knowledge of time and place
15. geography.

It is claimed to be an ideal pedagogical text – briefer, detailed according to the need, economical in statement and adorned with appropriate examples and it is urged that one who cannot analyse *kāvya* (verbal compositions) cannot properly understand the two elements of language – words and their meanings.

Typical of India's all intellectual traditions, literary thinking tradition is also a continuous and cumulative tradition of thinkers, texts and conceptual structures (theories). The primary texts, in spite of widespread historical loss and destruction, are still available and there is a fairly widespread agreement about the representative disciplines and texts of this tradition from second century BCE *Nāṭyaśāstra* to seventeenth-eighteenth century CE *Rasagaṅgādhara*. It is a tradition by virtue of continuity and cumulativeness of texts and thinkers; there is a source text, primary texts, *saṁgraha* texts, recensions, and a long line of commentaries, a powerful interpretive literature built around the primary texts. The commentaries serve to refine and extend the theory significantly so much so that the tradition regards the authoritative commentary and the primary text together as one source text for an area of knowledge, for example, *Dhvanyāloka-Locana* of Ānandavardhana–Abhinavagupta for the *dhvani* theory of literary meaning.

As the tradition is language-centred, the *śabda* (word) is crucial and interpretation is essentially a linguistic exegesis. The technical terms are almost always trans-disciplinary. *Rasa*, for example, is a category of chemistry, medicine, cooking and literary aesthetics. At another level, the eight *rasa*s of Bharata were sought to be reduced by later thinkers to one, ultimate *rasa* – *karuṇa, śṛṅgāra* or *śānta* – in the true spirit of monism. *Bhāva* is a construct in both philosophy and literary aesthetics. *Ātmasākṣātkāra* (self-realization) is a goal in philosophy, ritual, meditation and literary experience. Knowledge is not an end in itself – it justifies itself by upholding *dharma* or *ṛta* (the inherent equipoise in the individual, the society, the cosmos). In fact, the four ends of life laid down in the Dharmaśāstras (texts of sociology) constitute the goal of learning as well. So, command of both literature and language leads to *mokṣa* (liberation) from the self as much as the study of Vedas does.

We noted in the beginning that the Indian tradition is homogeneous in the sense that its single root is Vedic thought and literature. From this "root" have sprung diverse streams of philosophy, at least sixteen that are expounded by Śrī Madhvācārya in his thirteenth-century compendium of Indian philosophy, *Sarvadarśana Saṁgraha*. All the literary thinkers, poeticians, discuss and explain literary composition in the perspective of one or the other philosophy they subscribe to.

Unlike in the Western framework, theories of literature in Indian thought are not built around what are understood as the four components of literature – text, author, reader and context. Indian theories are constitutive theories built around compositional practices to explain how the verbal compositions are put together to mean what they variously mean to different readers. They explain how through words, clauses/sentences and various language-centred devices, the meaning and the effect of a litrary composition is constructed and achieved. That is, Indian theories are language-oriented theories and differ from each other in positing an overriding construct, an explanatory principle that is posited by the theory as the locus of literariness, the "soul" (*ātmā*) of the literary composition.

It is possible to classify the literary theories[5] on the basis of parts of composition which are central to them. Accordingly, we have a theory of:

---

[5] For a detailed discussion of Indian literary theories and thinking, see our book *Literary Theory: Indian Conceptual Framework.*

1. Language, namely, *alaṁkāra* (principle of figurativeness) and *vakrokti* (principle of deviation).
2. Style and compositional value, namely, *guṇa/doṣa* (excellence, faults), *rīti* (mode of expression) and *aucitya* (propriety).
3. Verbal symbolism, namely, *dhvani.*
4. Aesthetic experience, namely, *rasa.*
5. Narrative, namely, *mahāvākya,* as inferable from Bhoja's *Śṛṅgāraprakāśa* and categories of Pāṇini's grammar.
6. Discourse analysis, namely, *yuktis*. For example, Kauṭilya's thirty-two units of composition in *Arthaśāstra* (15.1). It is an analysis of the thought structure of a composition, constitution of a text in terms of the nature of propositions. Indian theorists do not explicitly discuss this but one can consolidate ideas available from different sources.
7. Comprehensive analysis (as constructed in *Kāvyamīmāṁsā*). Rājaśekhara has proposed a composite model based on the insights of different theories.

The seven recognized literary theory "schools" are given in Table 1.1. These are called schools (*sampradāya*) because each has: (i) a source, primary text, Śāstra, a teach-in-text, (ii) the first thinker, who enunciated the "theory" (*siddhānta*), and (iii) a line of thinkers who expounded and elaborated the theory. These are the three requirements for a set of ideas to be recognized as a distinct school of thought.

"Interpretation" may be considered as the eighth point of view. It is noteworthy that Indian literary theorists do not talk of interpreting the compositions. This is so because the tradition, as we have noted, opposes Śāstra and Kāvya, being Kāvya not subjected to serious interpretation – it is to be experienced and enjoyed. In the Śāstras, however, there is a powerful interpretive

Table 1.1: Major Theory Schools, Thinkers and Their Texts

School	*Thinker(s)*	*Text(s)*
Rasa	Bharata	*Nāṭyaśāstra* (second century BCE)
	Dhanika–Dhanañjaya	*Daśarūpaka* (tenth century CE)
Alaṁkāra	Bhāmaha	*Kāvyālaṁkāra* (sixth century CE)
	Daṇḍin	*Kāvyādarśa* (seventh century CE)
	Udbhaṭa	*Kāvyālaṁkārasāra Saṁgraha* (ninth century CE)
	Rudraṭa	*Kāvyālaṁkāra* (ninth century CE)
Rīti	Vāmana	*Kāvyālaṁkārasūtra* (ninth century CE)
Dhvani	Ānanda-vardhana	*Dhvanyāloka* (ninth century CE)
	Abhinavagupta	*Abhinavabhāratī* (also for *rasa* theory) (eleventh century CE) and *Locana* (commentary on *Dhvanyāloka*) (eleventh century CE)
	Mahimabhaṭṭa	*Vyaktiviveka* (eleventh century CE)
Vakrokti	Kuntaka	*Vakroktijīvita* (eleventh century CE)
Guṇa–Doṣa	Daṇḍin	*Kāvyādarśa* (listed above)
	Also Bhāmaha	*Kāvyālaṁkāra* (listed above)
Aucitya	Kṣemendra	*Aucityavicāracarcā* (eleventh century CE)

tradition and each Śāstra has a long line of exegetical commentaries. Consequently, there is a well-developed system of interpretation – *śāstrapaddhati* – which employs different interpretive instruments, including philosophy, grammar, etymology, logical reasoning, theory of meaning and meta-rules. There are powerful exegetes in the tradition – Śabara, Patañjali, Kumārila Bhaṭṭa, Śaṅkara and Rāmānuja. In case modern literary texts need to be interpreted, the system of interpretation available in the Śāstric tradition can be adopted and adapted not that there is no model of interpretation – only that interpretation has been restricted to Śāstras. We shall now briefly describe the major theories.

RASA

The *rasa* theory originates with Bharata in *Nāṭyaśāstra*. It claims that the object or meaning that is sought to be conveyed in literary compositions is in the nature of an emotional effect of diverse human experience on man's mind and heart. It is possible, Bharata demonstrates, to enumerate the whole range of emotions, or states, of being born of experience, and to analyse the structure of those emotions in terms of cause, physical correlation (effect) and their effect on man's being. The theory thus becomes in effect a theory of literary experience which is strongly rooted in the empirical human reality.

Bharata, the first enouncer of the theory, gives the most comprehensive analysis of its sources, nature and its categories. Subsequently, the theory found major commentators in Dhanika–Dhanañjaya who re-examined Bharata's typology of drama and added to it a typology of *uparūpaka*s, sub-plays, plays within plays and one-act plays. It is Abhinavagupta, however, who enriched the theory by elucidating its philosophic foundations and by analysing in depth the aesthetic dimension of the theory in terms of the nature, cognition and effect of literary experience.

The *rasa* theory has been accepted as the core literary theory by all major poeticians both before and after Abhinavagupta. In particular, the discussion and analysis by Viśvanātha and Pt. Jagannātha have contributed towards a more subtle understanding of *rasa* theory. This theory is discussed in Chapter 5.

ALAṀKĀRA

The earliest and most sustained school, it studies literary

language and assumes that the locus of literariness is in the figures of speech, in the mode of figurative expression, in the grammatical accuracy and pleasantness of sound (euphony). This does not mean that meaning is ignored. In fact, structural taxonomies of different figures of speech are models of how meaning is cognized and how it is to be extracted from the text. Bhāmaha (*Kāvyālaṁkāra*) talks of the pleasure of multiplicity of meaning inherent in certain *alaṁkāras* as *arthāntaranyāsa* (2.71), *vibhāvanā* (2.77) and *samāsokti* (2.79).

Bhāmaha is the first *ālaṁkārika* poetician. In chapters 2 and 3 of *Kāvyālaṁkāra*, he describes thirty-five figures of speech. Others who continued to the tradition are Daṇḍin, Udbhaṭa, Rudraṭa and Vāmana. Finally, in Ānandavardhana, *alaṁkāra* was sought to be integrated with *dhvani* and *rasa*. There is a form of suggestion (*dhvani*) which is evoked by figures of speech and which thus contributes to aesthetic experience (*rasa*).

The question is: is a figure of speech external to poetry (an ornament) or is it an integral part of conceptualization and of the way the poet visualizes? Metaphor, for example, relates to imaginative perception: "see how the moonlight sleeps on the bank". Is it the perception itself? Or, is it just one method of representing the perception? For Ruyyaka (*Alaṁkārasarvasva*), it may be noted, *alaṁkāra* is the *dharma* of poetry and not a mere embellishment (Dwivedi 1979: 57).

The categories of *alaṁkāra* have been classified by different poeticians into different kinds of systems. For example, Rudraṭa divides all *alaṁkāras* into two types – those based on phonetic form (*śabdālaṁkāra*) and those based on meaning (*arthālaṁkāra*) and then further subdivides each into five and four sub-types, respectively (see *fig.* 1.1).

Further subclassification of these leads to a total of sixty-eight *alaṁkāras*.

Bhoja did not provide a fresh classification but added the

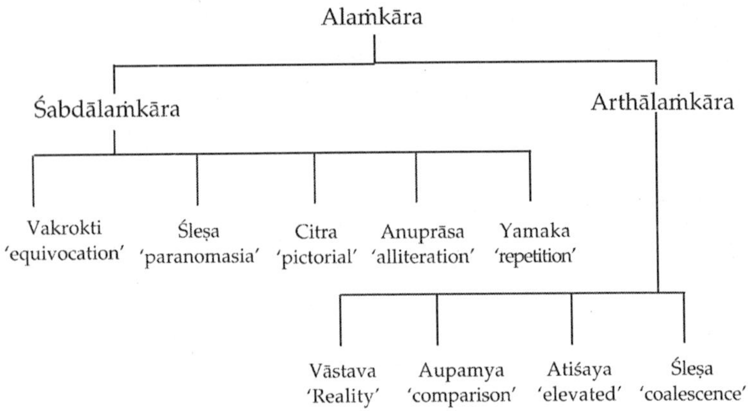

fig. 1.1: Rudraṭa's Classification

third category – *ubhayālaṁkāra* – to the two major types of Rudraṭa. Ruyyaka classified *alaṁkāras* into seven classes on the basis of their content (meaning), on the basis of how meaning is constituted:

1. *sādṛṣya* (similarity),
2. *virodha* (opposition),
3. *śṛṅkhalābaddha* (chain-bound),
4. *tarka nyāya* (reasoning, logic),
5. *lokanyāya* (popular logic),
6. *kāvyanyāya* (logic of poetry), and
7. *gūḍhārtha pratīti* (inference of meaning).

Mammaṭa enumerates sixty-one figures and groups them into seven types:

1. *upamā* (simile),
2. *rūpaka* (metaphor),
3. *aprastutapraśaṁsā* (indirect description),
4. *dīpaka* (stringed figures),
5. *vyatireka* (dissimilitude),
6. *virodha* (contradiction), and
7. *samuccaya* (concatenation).

In this way, the number of *alaṁkāras* identified increased from Bharata's original four to sixty-one enumerated by Mammaṭa. This taxonomy is not mere ingenuity; it represents global and local taxonomies, a refined analysis and classification of what ultimately are modes of perception. The different classificatory systems can be seen, based on the following parameters:

1. objects compared (*upameya*),
2. objects with which compared (*upamāna*),
3. value of figures,
4. semantic basis, such as similarity,
5. grammar (viz., *samāsokti*),
6. coherence with known facts or otherwise (*saṅgati*), and
7. syntax.

RĪTI

Rīti is a theory of language of literature. It is Vāmana who developed it into a theory, though it is described for the first time in Bharata's *Nāṭyaśāstra* under the rubric of *vṛtti*. As the theory of *viśiṣṭa padaracanā*, *Rīti* is a theory of formation of or arrangement of marked inflected constructions (*Kāvyālaṁkārasūtra* 1.2.6).

Table 1.2: Different Categories of Rīti

Theorist	*Categories*
Daṇḍin (*Kāvyādarśa* 1.39-105)	*Vaidarbhī, gauḍīya*
Vāmana (*Kāvyālaṁkārasūtra* 1.2.6-22)	*Vaidarbhī, gauḍīya, pāñcālī*
Kuntaka (*Vakroktijīvita* 1.24)	*Sukumāra, vicitra, madhyama* (*mārgas*)
Mammaṭa (*Kāvyaprakāśa*, chapter 8)	*Upanāgarika, prāsāda, komala*
Ānandavardhana (*Dhvanyāloka* 3.5, 46, 47)	*Samāsa, madhyamasamāsa, dīrghasamāsa*

Two other words used for *rīti* are *mārga* and *vṛtti*. Later Ānandavardhana (ninth century CE) distinguished these styles on the basis of the use of particular kinds of compounds. Daṇḍin uses the term *mārga* and talks of two *mārgas*. Mammaṭa designates the different modes as *vṛttis*. The different categories of *rīti* identified by different theorists are presented in Table 1.2.

*Rīti*s correlate with: (1) themes, (2) effect on the hearers/ viewers, and (3) sentiment (see *Kāvyaprakāśa* 8.77, *Dhvanyāloka* 3.33). Bharata (*Nāṭyaśāstra* 6.25) has all the three in mind in his discussion of *vṛtti*s: (1) Kaiśikī (for *śṛṅgāra*), (2) Bhāratī (for all *rasa*s), (3) Sāttavatī (for *vīra*), (4) Ārbhaṭī (for *raudra* and *bībhatsa*). Viśvanātha considers proper organization of language as *rīti* – words and phrases have to be properly selected and organized in poetry and this is necessary for *rasa*s and *bhāva*s. *Rīti*s (styles) are defined by *guṇa*s (excellences) as well (Viśvanātha, *Sāhitya-Darpaṇa*, chapters 8 and 9). *Rīti* may be called "diction", particularly when *guṇa/doṣa* become part of the discussion (*Sāhitya-Darpaṇa*, chapter 7), but *rīti* is much more than just diction. Basically, it is a theory that handles the psychophonetic fitness of language for speakers, themes and sentiments, and therefore becomes a study of craftsmanship and psychology of speech.

DHVANI

Next only to Rasa theory in importance, the Dhvani theory of Ānandavardhana considers suggestion, the indirectly evoked meaning, as the characteristic property of literary discourse, the determinant that separates it from other rational discourses. As articulated in *Dhvanyāloka*, *dhvani* becomes an all-embracing principle that explains the structure and function of the other major elements of literature – the aesthetic effect (*rasa*), the figural mode and devices (*alaṁkāra*), the stylistic values (*rīti*), and excellences and defects (*guṇa* and *doṣa*). All the subsequent literary theorists in the tradition found the combination of *rasa* and *dhvani* theories both adequate and sufficient to analyse the constitution of meaning in literature. In *Dhvanyāloka*, Ānandavardhana has presented a structural analysis of indirect literary meaning. He has classified different kinds of suggestion and defined them by identifying the nature of suggestion in each. In Todorov's view, Ānandavardhana "was perhaps the greatest of all theorists of textual symbolism" (1982: 12). The significance of Ānandavardhana's typology of verbal suggestion needs to be set out clearly. If we are able to explain how indirect meanings arise systematically, we are able to claim that all potential meanings are inherent in the text – all that the reader does is to exploit this system of verbal symbolism to construct a particular meaning. The text constitutes itself in each instance of reading no doubt, but, this constitution is based in a finite system. Ānandavardhana uses the term *dhvani* to designate the universe of suggestion – *kāvyasya ātmā dhvani* (*Dhvanyāloka* 1.1):

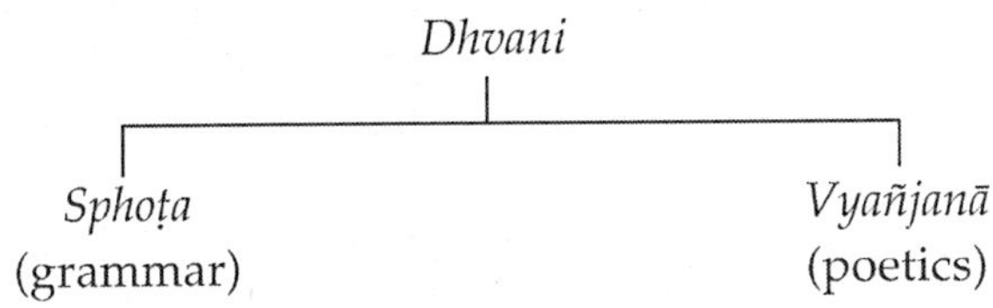

Ānandavardhana is openly indebted to Bhartṛhari's *sphoṭa* theory and he acknowledges it in *Dhvanyāloka* (1.13), where, as Krishnamoorthy (1981: 322-23) has explained, Ānandavardhana notes that he has chosen the term *dhvani* following the definite use of that term by the grammarians to denote (1) the sound structure of words (*śabda*), (2) the semantic aspect of *śabda*, the *vyañjakas* (suggesters), and (3) the revealed or suggested meaning as such and the process of suggestion involved (see Bhartṛhari, *Vākyapadīya* 1.47, 44, 102). *Dhvani* theory is a theory of meaning, of symbolism, and this principle leads to the poetry of suggestion being accepted as the highest kind of poetry.

Ānandavardhana proposes three levels of meaning – *abhidhā*, *lakṣaṇā* and *vyañjanā*. This is Ānandavardhana's contribution, to add the third level – rather, to split the indirectly expressed meaning into two. The *R̥gveda* also makes a distinction between the literal meaning and the inner significance – "He sees, but sees not . . . one hears, but hears not" (10.71.4). Besides literal meaning, there is socio-cultural meaning dependent on the contexts and emotions. The words, signs, are *vācaka* as well as *bodhaka*, i.e. expressive as well as indicatory signs, respectively. This *vyañjanā* (the tertiary meaning) may be communicated by words, sentences, discourse, contextual factors, intonation, gestures and even sounds. Another term used for *vyaṅgyārtha* (suggested meaning) is *pratīyamānārtha*:

> The meanings of sentences are determined according to the situation, word meaning, propriety . . . form. . . . Meaning depends on connection, separation, opposition, context, indication, the presence of another word . . . suitability.
>
> – Bhartr̥hari, *Vākyapadīya* 2.314-16

Ānandavardhana integrates *rasa* theory with his *dhvani* theory. *Dhvani* is the method, the means, for achieving or evoking *rasa*, which is the effect of suggestion.

Rasa is that constant aesthetic pleasure in all literature – its divisions are based on the *sthāyī bhāva*s which evoke the *rasa*s, states of mind. The *rasa* is a state or condition produced in the spectator, a single feeling, and a pleasurable one. It is generated by the interaction of *sthāyī bhāva* (relatively permanent emotional moods), *vibhāva* (substrate or "awakeners" of the emotions and the exciting causes and the contextual factors), *anubhāva* (external manifestations of the emotion) and *vyabhicārī bhāva*s (the ancillary or accessory emotions). Bharata's (*Nāṭyaśāstra* 6.32) *rasasūtra vibhāvanu-bhāva vyabhicārī saṁyogada rasaniṣpatti* has been interpreted differently from the points of view of (1) who is the substratum (*āśraya*) of *rasa*, (2) how it is generated, and (3) how it is experienced. Thus, it is argued that *rasa* exists in the hero/heroine (Lollaṭa). Further, it is suggested that the experience of *rasa* is a matter of inference (*śaṅkuka*). It is Bhaṭṭanāyaka who clearly asserts that *rasa* is experienced by the spectator, that it is the spectator's aesthetic experience, that the enjoyment of *rasa* is a subjective experience. Bhāṭṭnāyaka also distinguishes poetic language from ordinary language – the poetic language, besides *abhidhā* (primary meaning), has two other functions: (1) *bhāvakatva*, universalization or stripping *vibhāva* and *sthāyī bhāva* of individual and personal aspects, is the abstraction of the emotion, by the spectator, from its immediate location and context, and (2) *bhojakatva* (tasting or experiencing the emotion in one's self) consuming for oneself the emotion represented in the performance/text.

Abhinavagupta continues in the tradition of Bhāṭṭanāyaka in treating *rasa* experience as a cognitive process, but substituted for his *bhāvakatva* and *bhojakatva* the power of *vyañjanā* or *dhvani* (suggestion) in the context of the concepts of *prakāśa* (light) and *vimarśa* (consciousness). The three stages in the realization of *rasa* in literature, accordingly, are:

1. cognition of the formal, intellectual elements of the poem, a means to the second stage,
2. idealization of things in poetry or drama by the power of imagination in the reader/spectator,
3. intensification of the inexpressible effective (emotional) condition of the reader/spectator.

Finally, in the fourth stage, when the intellectual, the imaginative and the emotional responses blend into one predominant sentiment, and making a simultaneous appeal awaken the *sthāyī bhāva* of the reader/spectator, the taste of *rasa* is manifested as a unity in the heart leaving no trace of the constituent elements – that is why *rasa-dhvani* is called *asaṁlakṣyakrama vyaṅgya*, i.e. suggested sense with imperceptible stages.

The *dhvani* theory of meaning came in for criticism at the hands of Nyāya and Mīmāṁsā thinkers. The opponents said that (1) *dhvani* is non-existent, (2) *dhvani* is a product of inference and is to be included under *lakṣaṇa*, and (3) *dhvani* is something beyond the realm of words. Mahimabhaṭṭa (*Vyaktiviveka*) is the most well-known critic of this theory, but *dhvani* is not *lakṣaṇa* – it can be evoked by an idea, a figure of speech or even emotion. Even in the absence of *lakṣaṇa*, the word Gaṅgā can suggest purity and sanctity.

The goal is development of *rasa* – mere suggestion does not make poetry, for example, the use of "he is a villager" to suggest his non-urban manners. Ānandavardhana stresses the importance of taking the whole poem so that the overtones of the suggested sense are fully grasped. Isolated instances acquire full meaning in the context of the whole composition. (For Ānandavardhana's classification of *dhvani* categories, see *fig.* 1.2.)

The intonation adds a layer of suggested meaning to the directly expressed meaning of an utterance. Thus, the same sentence – he is a good man – can be uttered to assert disagreement with the proposition, interrogation.

It may be noted that the *dhvani* theorists enlarged the definition of *artha* to include all that a poem could mean or suggest – its cognitive, emotive, socio-cultural meanings depending on various factors besides the *abhidhārtha*. This also then leads to a classification of poetry in which *dhvani kāvya*, the poetry of suggestion, is considered supreme:

> The poetry in which the suggested meaning dominates the expressed, is poetry of the best kind, called *dhvani* by the learned. – Mammaṭa, *Kāvyaprakāśa* 1.4.

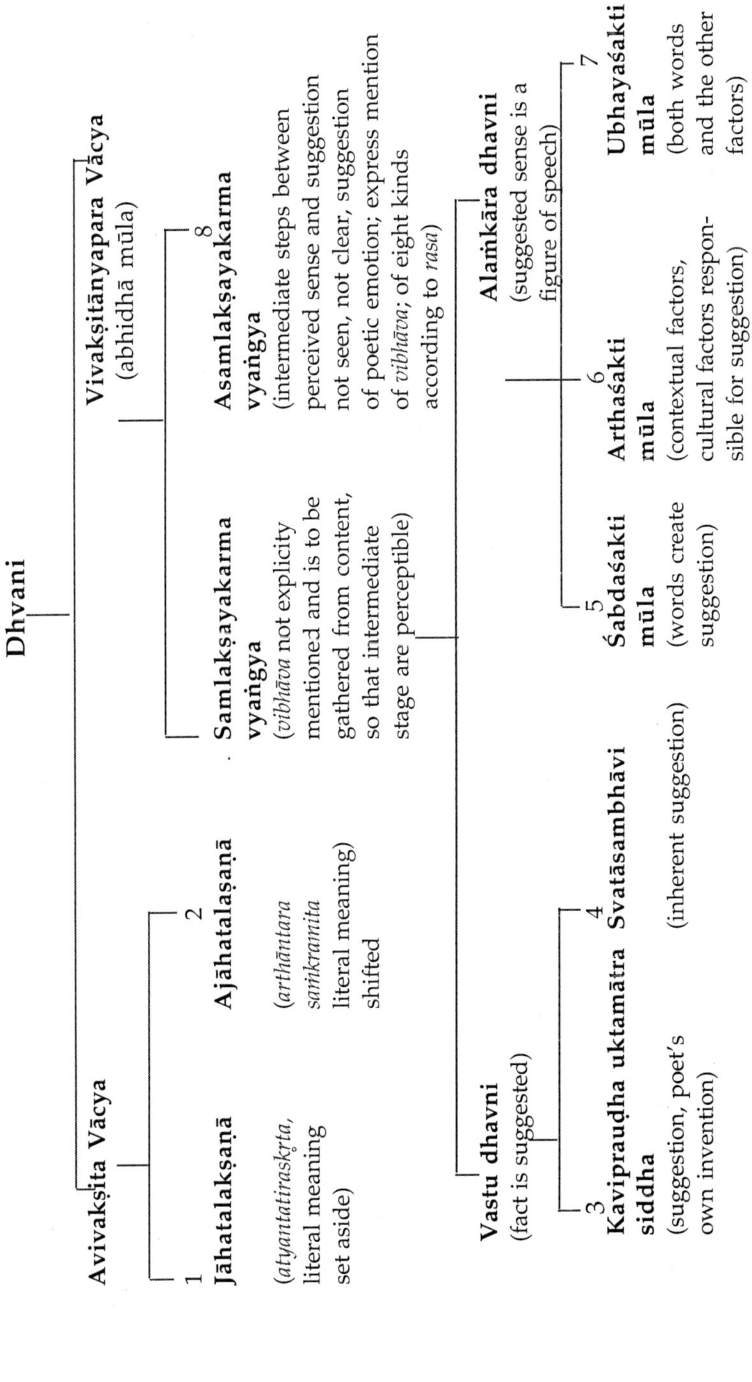

fig. 1.2 Classification of *dhvani* categories, according to Ānandavardhana

This focus on meaning and the type of meaning in poetry must be considered as a major contribution of Ānandavardhana to Indian literary theory. Further, the *dhvani* theory has both elucidated and strengthened the *rasa* theory, and the two together constitute a powerful explanatory framework. Finally, this theory of verbal symbolism enriched the Indian system of interpretation of texts (*artha nirdhāraṇa*) by making possible a method of symbol exegesis.

VAKROKTI

Vakrokti is also a theory of language of literature. It claims that the characteristic property of literary language is its "markedness". It deviates in identifiable ways from ordinary language in its form and in the way it constitutes meaning.

Kuntaka made *vakrokti* a full-fledged theory of literariness. He defines *vakrokti* as "both words and meanings marked by artistic turn of speech" (*Vakroktijīvita* 1.10). *Vakrokti* literally means *vakra ukti,* deviant or marked expression, and can also mean special denotation. It may be properly translated as "markedness". Kuntaka classifies *vakrokti* under six heads (*Vakroktijīvita* 1.18-21):

1. in syllables or their arrangements,
2. *bhānayaka* in the base substantives,
3. in inflected forms of substantives,
4. in sentences, including figures of speech,
5. in topics or sections, and
6. in the whole composition.

These cover the entire range of literary composition. What is the place of *mārga* (*rīti*) and *guṇa* in *vakrokti*? Kuntaka asks this question and says that the object of composition determines the *mārga* (mode). The three *mārga*s (styles) – *sukumāra* (elegant), *vicitra* (brilliant) and *madhyama* (the mixed or intermediate), as devices of expression – are to be treated as examples of *vakrokti* (*Vakroktijīvita* 1.24). Each has its qualities which Kuntaka delineates carefully (*Vakroktijīvita* 1.24-58). Six *guṇa*s (qualities) are identified in literary style: *aucitya* (propriety), *saubhāgya* (splendour), *mādhurya* (sweetness), *prāsāda* (perspicuity), *lāvaṇya* (grace) and *abhijātya* (classicality). These are defined as kinds of language used to achieve particular effects. In a similar vein, Kuntaka incorporates *rasa, alaṁkāra, rīti* and *guṇa* theories into his *vakrokti siddhānta*. *Vakrokti* was not discussed separately by later theorists but it has always been discussed as an important element. The principle of *vakrokti* has affinities with modern formalist theories of literature which consider the language of literature as deviant language. In the clarity of its conception and categories, *vakrokti* theory is a useful framework for stylistic analysis of literature.

GUṆA/DOṢA

This theory examines literary compositions in terms of qualities (*guṇa*) and defects (*doṣa*), both of form and meaning. From Bharata downwards every theorist has, more or less, concerned himself with this aspect of compositions. But it is Daṇḍin and, subsequently, Udbhaṭa who make *guṇa/doṣa* the primary features, the locus of literariness.

Bhāmaha, who was also a logician (*naiyāyika*), concerns himself only with defects. In two chapters (*Kāvyālaṁkāra*), he enumerates and discusses the general defects of expression and form (chapter 3) and the defects springing from failure of logical thinking (chapter 4). Vāmana (*Kāvyālaṁkārasūtra*) also concerns himself with ideal qualities of literary compositions (chapter 3) and the shortcomings, but for Vāmana, the defects (*doṣa*) are restricted to the figures of speech.

Daṇḍin takes a more wholistic view and assimilates the concepts of *rasa* and *rīti* in his conception of *guṇa* and *doṣa*. In this sense, in Daṇḍin, *guṇa* and *doṣa* are primary attributes of literary compositions. In chapter 1 of *Kāvyādarśa*, he discusses various qualities as attributes of *rīti*, and *rīti* for him is a method of expressing and evoking *rasa*, states of being. In the third chapter he discusses (1) logical failures, (2) linguistic failures, (3) failures of accurate reference to facts of life and world (*loka*), and (4) failure in communicating the described meanings. Daṇḍin, with a remarkable insight, then adds that through sheer originality and poetic power, any of these defects may be transformed into an excellence (*Kāvyādarśa* 3.179).

After Daṇḍin, Udbhaṭa correlates *guṇa/doṣa* with both *alaṁkāra* (figures of speech) and *rīti* (linguistic styles) and claimed that excellences and defects are not independent features which can be distinguished in isolation, in fact, *guṇa* and *doṣa* are properties of figural composition.

The *guṇa/doṣa* concept always remained an important component of literary theory but it did not acquire the status of a major literary theory that could account for all the aspects of literary composition — so did the tradition think.

AUCITYA

The theory of propriety or appropriateness claims that in all aspects of literary composition, there is the possibility of a perfect, the most appropriate choice – of subject, of ideas, of words, of devices. As such, it has affinities with Longinus' theory of the sublime, "On the Sublime". The concept of propriety with reference to custom, subject, character and sentiment recurs in almost all theorists and is often discussed in association with figures of speech, *guṇa/doṣa* and *rītis*. Ānandavardhana relates this principle specifically to *rasa* (*Dhvanyāloka* 3.7, 14). It has been used for propriety in delineating *bhāvas* according to characters, and in the choice of *mārgas* (for example, in the use of compounds) according to the speaker, content and type of literary composition. Kṣemendra made *aucitya* the central element of literariness. He defines *aucitya* as the property of an expression (signifier) being an exact and appropriate analogue of the expressed (signified) (*Aucityavicāracarcā*, verse 6). For Kṣemendra, *aucitya* is the *ātmā* (soul) of literature. What is the value of artifaces of language and images, and figures of speech, if *kāvya* does not teach *jīvana-aucitya* – the value of propriety in life?

In verses 8-10 of *Aucityavicāracarcā*, Kṣemendra enumerates the areas, locations or sites of literary compositions where the concept of *aucitya* is pertinent:

1. *pada* (phrase),
2. *vākya* (sentence),
3. *prabandhārtha* (meaning in whole composition),
4. *guṇa* (excellence, quality),
5. *alaṁkāra* (poetic figure),
6. *rasa* (state of being),
7. *kāraka* (case-ending),
8. *kriyā* (verb),
9. *liṅga* (gender or marking),
10. *vacana* (number),
11. *viśeṣaṇa* (qualification),
12. *upasarga* (prefix),
13. *nipāta* (redundancies),
14. *kāla* (time, tense),
15. *deśa* (country),
16. *kula* (family),
17. *vrata* (custom),
18. *tattva* (truth),
19. *sattva* (inherent self),
20. *abhiprāya* (motive),
21. *svabhāva* (nature),
22. *sāra saṁgraha* (essential property),
23. *pratibhā* (innate ability),
24. *avasthā* (condition, state),
25. *vicāra* (thought),
26. *nāma* (name), and
27. *āśīrvāda* (blessings).

These are the limbs or constituents of a literary composition, according to Kṣemendra, and belong to different levels or domains of language, ideas, creativity, encyclopaedic information, poetic devices and grammar.

Like *guṇa/doṣa*, *aucitya* also did not prevail as an independent literary theory, but remained with every subsequent theorist as an important principle. Kṣemendra's contribution in constituting this principle is clear and definite.

It may be noted that Kṣemendra's discussion of the principle of *aucitya* is from the point of view of both the writer and the reader, and is articulated in its given cultural and philosophical context.

We may as well list here the major *saṁgraha* texts, compendiums that classify all thoughts into issues of theory and, on each issue, put critically together what all primary thinkers thought about that issue. These are the important *saṁgraha* texts:

Thinker	*Text(s)*
Rājaśekhara	*Kāvyamīmāṁsā* (ninth century CE)
Bhojarāja	*Sarasvatīkaṇṭhābharaṇa*, *Śṛṅgāraprakāśa* (eleventh century CE)
Mammaṭa	*Kāvyaprakāśa* (eleventh century CE)
Viśvanātha	*Sāhitya-Darpaṇa* (fourteenth century CE)

Indian literary theories are constitutive theories, i.e. they are concerned with analysing how meaning is constructed, through devices of cognition and communication, and how the work succeeds in giving enjoyment, *ānanda*, to the *sahṛdaya*s. There is a pervasive consciousness of the linguistic materiality of texts and a concern for craftsmanship and form, as it is believed that it is HOW something is constructed that constitutes the element of beauty in a composition and is the source of delight. The major concern, therefore, is chiefly HOW and secondarily WHAT (meaning) to the extent that "what" is involved in explaining "how". This explains the exhaustive enumeration and examination of *alaṁkāras*, the figures of speech – a subject that remains central throughout the tradition of literary thinking. These devices are not seen as merely "ornaments" but as integral to the constitution of meanings – as the poet's epistemology, his mode of perception. Many *rasa* theorists, who assume that the aesthetic experience itself is an objective fact, and therefore it is possible and desirable to explain objectively why people enjoy and what they enjoy, explained objectively literary experience, *rasa*. The enjoyment (*ānanda*) is sought to be located by many theorists in the craft of language, the rhetoric of composition. The attempt is to concretize it by showing how it emanates from the constituted text and its realization even when the experience is accepted as subjective.

The Indian poeticians are able to carry out extremely refined analysis of and discrimination between various *alaṁkāras*[6] because of the long pre-existing traditions of thought – etymology, grammar, philosophy and logic (Nirukta, Vyākaraṇa, Darśana and Nyāya). All the three traditions investigated the questions of word–meaning relationship, and the nature and cognition of word meaning (*śabdaśakti* and *śābdabodha*)[7] in their specific contexts. The poeticians use the categories developed in other disciplines. Consider, for example, Mammaṭa's definition and discussions of contradiction (*virodha*) in terms of categories such as universal (*jāti*), particular (*vyakti*), quality (*guṇa*), substance (*dravya*) and action (*kriyā*):

---

6 Not counting the subtypes. Mammaṭa (*Kāvyaprakāśa*, chapter 10) reports and exemplifies sixty-one different figures (*alaṁkāras*).

7 Bhāmaha (*Kāvyālaṁkāra*, chapters 4-5), for example, discusses the shortcomings in compositions in terms of the validity of their propositions *vis-à-vis* the propositions in different systems of knowledge, e.g. Nyāya (logic), Āgama (Vedas).

> When something is spoken of as contradictory, even when there is no contradiction, it is the figure contradiction.
>
> (1-4) The universal contradicted by the four, (1) universal, (2) quality, (3) action, and (4) substance. (5-7) The quality contradicted by three (i.e. quality, action and substance). (8-9) The action contradicted by two, i.e. action and substance. (10) The substance contradicted by substance; thus this figure is often of ten kinds. – *Kāvyaprakāśa* 10.166-67

Non-isolation of disciplines is an evident fact of the Indian intellectual tradition and characterizes Indian literary thought as well. However, Kāvyaśāstra, on account of its awareness of the linguistic materiality of compositions, draws its inspiration from and is rooted in the Indian linguistic tradition, particularly Vyākaraṇa, which is among the earliest fields of study to become a Śāstra (Pāṇini's *Aṣṭādhyāyī* is seventh century BCE).[8] Bhāmaha (*Kāvyālaṁkāra* 6.62-63), an early poetician, pays obeisance to the grammarians, particularly Pāṇini, and discusses the language of literary composition in terms of the categories of grammar (root, compound, adverbial, affix, etc.). Bhāmaha also discusses the nature of lexical denotation and disputes the Buddhist theory of *anyāpoha* (6.16-19) on the ground that the theory predicates about the meaning of words, differentiation *apavāda* first and then affirmation *vidhi* which is contrary to ordinary experience in which there is first produced the idea of something affirmative and it is by/after/from this that the word becomes capable of excluding other things.

---

[8] The dates are neither definite nor really pertinent in Indian thought – "beforeafter" disposition of thinkers is taken note of and is relevant. Dates of thinkers and texts are arrived at on the basis of information inside the text and references to the text in other works, and some principles of judgement. For example, it is believed that not to mention Buddha is not to have known him, and not to have known Buddha is to have been born before him. This argument is used to place Pāṇini before Buddha.

2

Theory of Literature

THEORY of literature asks and answers general questions about literature such as what are the properties common to all literature? What is the function of literature? What different forms does literature take? What is the nature of literary creativity? What are the elements of form and meaning in different kinds of literary compositions? What is the nature of literary meaning? What is the relationship between a literary composition and (a) its author, (b) its readers, (c) its age and context? All these "principles and criteria of literature", we have said, constitute the domain of poetics.

In this chapter, we will restrict ourselves to the following key issues that are, and have been, discussed by literary thinkers through ages:

1. Definition of Literature
2. Nature of Literature
3. Goal of Literature
4. Role of Literature in Society
5. Literature as Mimetic Art
6. Literature as Discourse of Knowledge
7. Creativity and Creative Process

Definition of Literature

The word "literature" is a fourteenth-century borrowing from Latin *literatura*, itself derived from *litera*, letter. It has several interrelated meanings:

1. Written material, such as novels, poems and plays, that is valued for its language and content.
2. The whole body of written works of a particular country or period in time of American literature.
3. The whole body of information published on a particular subject of scientific literature.
4. The art or works produced by a writer.

And, now, colloquially, any printed matter, especially advertising leaflets.

Clearly "literature" in the Western tradition stands for "written compositions". There is in that tradition an ancient respect for the script and an ancient value of the written word – in the beginning there was the "word". The Greeks worshipped their script and in the contiguous Hebraic world, when Moses went up the Mount Sinai and conversed with God who came down to give him the injunctions, Moses pleaded with him to put down his Ten Commandments in writing and God engraved them on stone with his "hand of fire". The Greeks were oral people who composed epics and plays to be sung by the rhapsodist and performed by actors, an essentially aural–visual experience. Homer was a poet of orality – but soon the civilization took a turn with the Romans – and Virgil as the poet of a written culture. "Literature" henceforth is of "letters", compositions that exist in letters.

The corresponding Indian word is *vāṅgmaya* from *vākmaya* = "that is permeated by speech", i.e. all compositions in (language) the spoken word. *Kāvya* (literature) in Indian culture is essentially oral, an artefact in the spoken word. The metropolitan literature composed under the impact of the British rule is literature written by English-educated Indians in English and in major Indian languages and is different from the massive body of mainstream oral literature in numerous

Indian languages in its urban civilization-centred themes and in its philosophy and goal.

It is difficult to unambiguously define "literature". All the different markers, defining parameters, beg questions in turn. Literature, it is said, encompasses works of "imagination" – but what is "imagination"; and, moreover, is imagination not involved more or less in all writing, including history and philosophy? Its content is "fiction" as against "fact", another argument runs – but are "facts" also not just constructions like fiction as many history narratives have strong elements of fiction in them. Sometimes there is infinite regress in the effort to define as when we say literature is what "writers" compose and then in turn define "writers" as those who compose literature.

In the Indian discussions, *kāvya* derivationally means the work or deed of a *kavi* (poet). What is the work or deed of a *kavi*? A charming, out of the ordinary use of words, to describe something or some meaning is the work or deed of a poet. Since the *kavi*'s deed is in words (*śabda*) it may be said that *kāvya* is *śabda*, a creation in language. This is the most general definition. There is however some specificity about literature being definable in terms of the characteristics of a *kavi*. The word *kavi* in its two possible derivations (from √*kəv* and from √*kuṅ*, respectively) means (1) one who describes an object, and (2) one who talks about/uses words about a subject. In *Amarakośa* (2.7.5), for *vidvān*, *kavi* is a synonym along with *paṇḍita*, one who knows Śāstras, has discriminating intellect, and *maniṣī* (a thoughtful) meditative person. So *kavi* is a learned man who describes some subject/object. Under this definition, the ultimate reality, *paramātmā*, is also designated as *kavi*. Also, Brahmā, the source of Vedas, is described as *ādikavi* (*Bhagavad-Gītā*). Next, Vālmīki, the composer of *Rāmāyaṇa*, in the language of the people (*laukika-bhāṣā*), is also called *ādikavi*. Thereafter the learned composer of *Mahābhārata* and Purāṇas is described as a *kavi*. The title is then extended to all those who describe something, so that even Śukrācārya, the composer of a text on polity (*Nītisāra*), is called *kavi* (*Amarakośa* 1.3.25). Literature in this perspective is a learned discourse. More of it will come later.

All *vāṅgmaya* is a statement of "all this" (reality, creation, objects of knowledge). *Kāvya* means compositions dealing with themes, events and ideas locally realized in the understanding of one individual or individuals. Epics, Purāṇas, narrative poems and prose narratives belong to this category. *Kit* literally means "composed". Pāṇini, the great grammarian, mentions imaginative compositions (*ākhyāyikas*) and poetical compositions in two separate *sūtras*: 4.3.87 and 4.3.116. *Kāśikā*, a seventh-century commentary on *Aṣṭādhyāyī*, mentions narratives dealing with the life and times of the noble rulers of men, Yayāti, Subhadrā, etc. The epic *Mahābhārata* is explicitly mentioned by Pāṇini in *sūtra* 4.2.38. *Kāvya* compositions belong to this category.

The Indian poeticians have enumerated the properties of, and defined, literary composition. The definitions fall into the following groups in terms of:

1. language of composition (*śabda*);
2. meaning (*artha*);
3. figurative device (*alaṁkāra*); and
4. literary experience (*rasa*).

These may be further reduced to two major divisions:

1. definitions in terms of craft and representation (*dehavādī*, believers in form); and
2. definitions in terms of substance or content or experience represented (*ātmavādī*, believers in substance or meaning).

An examination of these definitions shows the following gradual evolution of the concept of *kāvya*:

1. *Agni Purāṇa* defines *kāvya* as a sequence of words that expresses the desirable meaning with brevity, devoid of faults, possessed of excellence and figurative devices. There is no redundancy in expression and the goal is to communicate some worthy meaning.

2. Bharata's description of ideal composition has six elements (*Nāṭyaśāstra* 17.121): sweet and transparent words; absence of esoteric words and esoteric ideas; easy to see, understand and enjoy; presence of integral elements of dance; continuous evocation of a state of mind (*rasa*); and properly arranged, organized content. This comprehensive statement is the source of later discussions.

3. For Bhāmaha, "word and meaning (*śabdārtha*) together (*sahitau*) constitute *kāvya*" (*Kāvyālaṁkāra* 1.16) and its utterances are "characterized by indirectness (*vakratā*)" (*Kāvyālaṁkāra* 1.30). This rejects both the exclusivist positions – that *kāvya* is a special language or just as special meanings. It suggests oneness of words and meaning, such that one cannot think of words or meaning separately, in isolation from the other. This integration became the basis later for the use of the word *sāhitya* for literary compositions. *Śabda* is the cardinal element in the Śrutis and *artha* in the Smṛtis. Bhāmaha defines literary discourse as one in which both *śabda* and *artha* are important – of course, different now, in their fancifulness or charm, i.e. *vakratā*.

4. Vāmana adds a new element, *alaṁkāra – kāvyam grāhyam alaṁkāratā* (*Kāvyālaṁkārasūtra* 1.1.1-2), i.e. literary compositions include that which is marked by embellishment. *Saundarya* (beauty) is *alaṁkāra*, i.e. embellishment, which is a rhetorical property for Vāmana and a matter of craft. Vāmana is the first to specifically mention "beauty" in the context of literary

compositions.

5. Rudraṭa follows Vāmana but extends the notion of creativity, specific so far to the language of *kāvya*, to meaning as well – literary meaning is the poet's creation so that even historic personages when they figure in a literary composition become the poet's creation and are not the same as actual historical personages. Pr̥thvīrāja of *Pr̥thvīrājarāso* is of course the Pr̥thvīrāja of Kilā Rāī Pithoṛā of Delhi but understandably the poetic personage cannot be construed as identical with the historical personage.

6. Ānandavardhana's contribution is the concept of *dhvani* – in a literary composition, he says, the meaning is always indirectly expressed (*Dhvanyāloka* 1.1). He subscribes otherwise to the view that word and meaning together constitute *kāvya*: *śabdārtha śarīram tāvatakāvyam* (*Dhvanyāloka* 1.1). Mammaṭa later classifies and grades poetry according to suggestion, *dhvani* (*Kāvyaprakāśa* 1.4, 4.2-4). We also see Viśvanātha's fourfold division of *kāvya* into excellent, superior, medium and low (*Sāhitya-Darpaṇa*, chapter 1).

7. Kuntaka introduced the concept of *vakratā* (*Vakroktijīvita* 1.7) – archedness of both expression and meaning marks literary compositions. His contribution is this concept of deviation from the norm at different levels of language, composition and theme.

8. Bhoja introduces the notion of absence of *doṣa* (faults) and of poetry endowed with *guṇas*. He otherwise subscribes to the *śabdārtha* view and holds that *alaṁkāras*, both *śabda* and *artha*, are indispensable elements of *kāvya*. He also includes *rasa* (*Śr̥ṅgāraprakāśa*, chapter 1).

9. Mammaṭa exalts absence of *doṣa*s (faults) and presence

of *guṇas* (excellence) (*Kāvyaprakāśa* 1.4). He reduces the importance of *alaṁkāras* – they may at times be absent (*Kāvyaprakāśa* 1.4). *Guṇas* are, for Mammaṭa, the attributes of *rasa*.

10. Viśvanātha's contribution is that he made *rasa* the pre-eminent, in fact, the sole determinant of *kāvya* which he defines as sentences (*vākya*) infused with *rasa*.
11. Finally, Pt. Jagannātha identifies the element of *ramaṇīya artha* (charming meaning) in literary compositions: "Verbal discourse that communicates/establishes charming meaning is *kāvya*" (*Rasagaṅgādhara*, chapter 1). What is "charming meaning"? That which produces in the hearer/experiencer extraordinary delight (*lokottarāhlāda*).

Nature of Literature

In the Indian context of orality, literature has been an act of public communication, a performance. This is why all literature is classified either as *śravya* (aural) or as *prekṣā* (visual) or as *śravya–prekṣā* (aural–visual). This fact of oral, folk literary practices determines the nature of compositions, the relationship of literary compositions to the audience/viewer/reader and therefore the concepts of literary theory. In this context the word "literature" itself is only partly appropriate for literature is of letters, the visible marks on the page and hence the notion that everything in print is literature. We define literature in one of the ensuing sections; suffice it to say here that they are compositions, and for the poet/writer, the term "composer" is more appropriate as it quite rightly evokes associations of (classical European) music, as a poet is like a musician in that part where his art lies in shaping sounds, or the speech sounds. Again, we cannot use the word "reader" – should we say "audience", "participant", "hearer" or "viewer"? Perhaps the Indian term *sahṛdaya*, the same kind of heart, i.e. one who is able to empathize, is a satisfactory term. It creates an entity that is more fluid and is richer. A *sahṛdaya* has the competence analogous to that of the poet/composer to see, to hear, to feel, to participate, to experience.

The oral tradition also determines the nature and character of compositions. It is a tradition of recounting – hence, a considerable part of Indian literature is some form of *kathā* (narrative).

If we divide all compositions into two sets – (1) of being, and (2) of becoming, the descriptive–theoretic writing versus the narrative composition, one essentially with narrative stasis and the other moving dynamically and temporarily from one state of existence to another and if we accept this division, we may say that all literary compositions are essentially "narrative". There is always change and substitution – be it a poem, a play, a story. There is disturbance and flux, and the resolution is always the creation of a new structure. Narratives are epigrams of transience and evoke insecurity and unease because they conceptualize and articulate the fragility and the instability of life. Hence the imperative to replace them by something more stable, more typical. For example, the special narrative mode in classical and in oriental civilizations – the mythical mode – which eliminates "the local habitation and name" from the record and transforms the events into a paradigm. The Purāṇas are theories, i.e. abstracted (permanent) structures from purely temporal and particular accidents and events. The same narratives are told and retold in the folk as well as literary manner, in verse and in prose, and the narrative preponderates as a form. But the narrative and the dramatic interact, the visual and the aural coexist, in all compositions. The Indian literary theory in its general principles and in its categories is a response to these oral compositions which seek to involve the hearer/viewer emotionally or rather inform him – for notice that the story is generally familiar and it is not the event or what is to happen next that is of interest to the audience. It is the particular enactment, the representation, which is of interest and it is successful to the extent it reinterprets and is able to evoke the "feel" of the experience in the viewer/hearer. The familiarity of the story decontextualizes it and in its rambling movement of a tale within a tale, its philosophizing, and its strung on episodes, it takes the audience through a whole range of emotions. The *rasa* theory is an inference from this body of compositions.

Aristotle uses the word "poetry" where we are using "literature" and treats major forms as different arts:

> Epic poetry and tragedy, as also comedy, dithyrambic poetry, and most flute-playing and lyre-playing, are all, viewed as a whole modes of imitation . . . differ[ing] from one another in their ways, either by a difference of kind in their means, or by differences in the objects, or in the manner of their imitations.

The characterization of literature or arts as "modes of imitation" defines literature in terms of the creativity involved and as such belongs to our subsequent discussion of literary creativity.

The thinking about literature among the Greeks is monolingual for they have only the Greek compositions as their object. But the Indian thinking has all through been multi-lingual/ethnic/cultural, as attested in eighth-century Rājaśekhara's characterization of Indian literatures in his image of the *kāvya-puruṣa*. The whole compositional literature is visualized as a *puruṣa*[1], a person, in human form:

> *Words* and *meaning* together constitute its substance.

[1] To see something in the human shape is a device used to conceptualize the structure and spread of an entity. In *Bhagavad-Gītā* the same device is used to communicate the concept of *Brahman* as *virāṭa-rūpa*.

> Sanskrit language is its mouth. Prākṛts are its arms. Apabhraṁśas, its thighs. Paiśācī language, its feet and mixed languages its chest.[2] Even/honest (*sama*), pleasant (*prasanna*), melodious (*madhura*), extensive/liberal (*udāra*), vigorous (*ojasun*) – these are your attributes. Metre, your pores. Question followed by an answer, conundrum or quiz, problem – these are your modes. *Anuprāsa* (alliteration/repetition), *upamā* (simile) and such other devices ornament you. Even Śruti, dealing with ultimate meanings, praises you.
>
> – Rājaśekhara, *Kāvyamīmāṁsā*, chapter 3

Apart from defining in a straightforward manner, the attributes of *kāvya* (*guṇa*s, metre, *rasa*, figural devices, exalted language and forms), this image captures the spread of compositional literature and attests the existence of such literature in almost all languages of India, distributed geographically as well as in the vertical clins of extent. Reference has been made to compositions even in the intermediate dialects. Daṇḍin in *Kāvyādarśa* (1.37) also refers to compositions in languages other than Sanskrit.

Next, the brief episode of Sarasvatī, the goddess of learning, leaving this world and going to the nobler realm of *brahmaloka* and leaving her son, the *kāvyapuruṣa*, behind in this world shows that *kāvya* is essentially worldly (ostensibly this distinguishes *kāvya* from both Śruti and Smṛti which are strongly oriented towards *jñāna* (knowledge)). The separation from the goddess of learning means a separation from *brahmavidyā* (higher forms of knowledge). Sarasvatī tells *kāvyapuruṣa* that his going to *brahmaloka* will not be appropriate. Thus separated from Sarasvatī, *kāvyapuruṣa* is wedded to the

---

2 Prākṛt refers to Mahārāṣṭrī. Apabharaṁśa is *deśabhāṣitam* the spoken language of the ordinary people; Paiśācī is the later form of north-western Prākṛt, in the region of Afghanistan and territories west of the river Indus. Mixed languages are the intermediate dialects (see Gune 1970: 234).

bride *sāhitya vidyā* (literary study; aesthetics). *Kāvya* thus broke off from Vedas, in its purpose and structure.

Rājaśekhara then dwells on the regional character and properties of different Indian literatures. The *kāvyapuruṣa* and his bride, *sāhitya vidyā* (poetics) together, we are told, roamed all over. It is obvious they started their journey from the middle country, the heartland, the area around Ujjain, where it is suggested the earliest *kāvya* literature originated. They travelled East (and a number of recognizable territories of the East (Prācya) are mentioned) and shaped and influenced the dress habits (*pravṛtti*), song and music (*vṛtti*) and the literary practice *rīti* of the eastern peoples. Now this is interesting. What does this mean, this shaping of dress, song/music and literary compositions? Evidently it is drama (*nāṭya*) that Rājaśekhara has in mind – drama has all these elements and more (eleven, in all, *vide* Bharata, *Nāṭyaśāstra* 6.23). Through drama, the dress habits, the song and music and the literary practices of the Madhyadeśa (region comprising contiguous borders of Uttar Pradesh, Madhya Pradesh and Maharashtra in Rājaśekhara's time) travelled east and interacting with local habits and traditions produced a recognizable form of what one terms as the culture of eastern India. In literary practice, this *rīti* (literary mode) is called *Gauḍīya rīti* (dress habits of the east) and the modes of song and dance are termed Auḍra Māgadhī and Bhāratī *vṛtti*, respectively.

Narration of their travels to north-west is then picked up followed by those to the south (Dākṣiṇātya), north-west (Udīcya) literary mode is identified as Pāñcālī Rīti, that of the central-southern India (Vidarbha) which was identified by Vāmana as the strong, simple, elegant style (*Kāvyālaṁkārasūtra* 1.2.11, 20).

This division of the subcontinent into three cultural zones is a very ancient division. Some major texts, in fact, come in three recensions corresponding to these three divisions –

Udīcya (north-west), Prācya (eastern), Dākṣiṇātya (southern). Thus, *Mahābhārata* comes in three *pāṭhas* (recensions). A preliminary application of the categories of *rīti* school shows that many attributes of these three *rīti*s are identifiable in the language habits of the speakers of even modern Indian languages in these three regions.[3]

From the point of view of dress and dance and music, Rājaśekhara divides the subcontinent into four parts: east, north-west, central and southern, with territories and regions of each zone clearly identified. From the point of view of properties of composition, however, there are only three zones. A question is understandably asked – as regions and regional identities are so many, how can they all be subsumed under four kinds? The answer is significant. This whole country is *cakravartī kṣetra,* and small internal differences mark numerous regions. A *cakravartin* is a centrally administered/administrable unit – like the structure of a wheel (*cakra*). It also means then, by extension, a *rāṣṭra* (country). This transcendental concept is the answer to the visible ethnography of India – and the word *rāṣṭra* in this sense is employed as early as the *Atharvaveda* (Pr̥thvī-Sūkta, 12.1.8). A division into four zones is practical and adequate. The overall cultural unity of this country results from the fact that cultural modes originate in one area and then spread over all the regions in which they are articulated in close interaction with local modes and manners. In the ninth century CE, the culture of Vidarbha – overlapping parts of modern Andhra Pradesh, Madhya Pradesh and Maharashtra – provided the norm for dress, song, drama

---

3 At the level of parts of speech, for example, it has been said that the Dākṣiṇātya (southern) mode prefers *taddhita* forms (secondary derived nominals), *pratyaya* (affix), *dīrghasamāsa* (long compounds); and Udīcya (north-western India), *ākhyāta* (verbs). A controlled, quantitative analysis to investigate this would be interesting.

and other literary compositions.

Goal of Literature

At the root of Greek thought, Socrates/Plato averred that art must educate by entertaining. The artists must portray the "essential" reality to educate its audience. But what the artist does create is in fact only an image – a phantasm, a mere semblance, a "fictional" reality and "not" ideational. Plato thus makes a clear distinction between the ideational and the fictional. The "fictional" has its existence at the "visible" level. In fact, the poet imitates, not even the idea – he imitates/ images the "object" and therefore creates only shadows (at the level of appearance). On this count, in Book X of *The Republic,* Plato makes a fundamental objection to literature. The poet imitates the objects and other visible phenomena of the world around him – it is like, says Plato, a mirror being turned round and round in all directions. (This image of the mirror became a part of the vocabulary of the theory of mimetic realism; for example, "literature mirrors life".) But the tangible objects are themselves images of certain conceptual forms (which in turn are images of the transcendental ideational realities). Thus in Plato's scheme of things, artistic/poetic creation has a very low truth value – it is an imitation of an imitation and is, therefore, thrice removed from reality. As such, literature is not a valid means of knowledge. This is reinforced in "Ion", in which Plato argues that the poet is not in control of his creative act but is an instrument for an agency outside himself. Again since literary creation is a product of a spell of madness, it can lay no claim to being a rational discourse, to being a statement of "knowledge". The poet who casually speaks of so many things with apparent authoritativeness is being too presumptuous.

But more than the philosophic (the ontological and the epistemological) objection to literary representation, it is the doubtful ethical value and the emotional effect of literature that Plato finds most harmful both for social systems and individuals. Plato admits the aesthetic joy that literature provides and is aware that drama is enjoyable and popular and therefore widely effective. It must therefore be rejected because the spectacle of unrestrained emotion is morally damaging to the ideal reader who must, desirably, cultivate restraint and fortitude. Thus literary value is ethical and social (ideological) rather than aesthetic in Plato. It is also a recognition of the fact that literature is (or can be) an effective propaganda, and not necessarily a repository of unquestionable absolute values.

Art must educate people in truth and moral values in Plato's view, which unfortunately it does not. Aristotle disagreeing with Plato argues that literature teaches "poetic truth" which is superior to both philosophic and historical truth. Aristotle reverses the paradigm – the historian

> describes the thing that has been, and the (poet) a kind of thing that might be. Hence poetry is something more philosophic and of graver import than history, since its statements are rather of the nature of universals, whereas those of history are singulars. – Section 9

Evidently, the goal of art for the Greeks is ethical. In recent times, this purposefulness of art was briefly questioned by the aestheticism of nineteenth-century Europe that argued that the goal of art is purely aesthetic, "art for art's sake", but it was soon overtaken by affectivist thought arguing moral, social, utilitarian or political goals.

In the Indian thought, there is prolonged meditation on the purpose/goal of literary compositions (*kāvyaprayojana*). The definitions of literature draw attention to the elements of craft and the elements of meaning such that they "delight" the hearer/viewer/participant. This leads to the question – what is the purpose of *kāvya*? Properties or attributes correlate with purpose. Now the tradition once again is quite comprehensive and typically offers more than one answer, but broadly the answers encompass both delight (*ānanda*) and eradication of ignorance (*avidyā*) which is the root cause of sorrow in the dominant Indian view. Second, when the theorists talk of the purposes of *kāvya*, they sometimes have the makers of *kāvya* in mind and sometimes the receivers of *kāvya*. In the Indian context, all worldly and spiritual pursuits are measured by their role/contribution in the attainment of *puruṣārtha*, the four ends of life – *dharma* (righteousness), *artha* (worldly prosperity), *kāma* (satisfaction of desires) and *mokṣa* (liberation from sorrows). No activity is an end in itself – not even acquiring knowledge. So quite a few Indian texts open with an invocation to Goddess Sarasvatī, seeking a fulfilment of worldly desires and supraworldly happiness.

This applies to *kāvya* as well. The discussions of purpose are carried out from different perspectives – the poet, the experiencer or audience, social life, the world-view or philosophy of life.

Bharata, talking of dramaturgy, says this is the "fifth" Veda (branch of knowledge) and it ensures "righteousness, good reputation, long life, well-being, increase in mental ability" and provides "guidance to ordinary people in the conduct of life [and also help them] have serious thoughts (*śāstrīya artha*)" (*Nāṭyaśāstra* 1.14-15).

Bhāmaha says:

> Composition of good poetry produces, also in arts, ability in *dharma*, *artha*, *kāma* and *mokṣa*. It also confers pleasure and fame. – *Kāvyālaṁkāra* 1.2

Vāmana says:

> Poetry, when excellent, accomplishes perceptible as well as

> imperceptible results, bringing about as it does pleasure and fame. – *Kāvyālaṁkārasūtra* 1.1.5

Mammaṭa gives these purposes of *kāvya*:

> *Kāvya* brings fame and riches, knowledge of the ways of the world and relief from evils, instant and perfect happiness (*ānanda*), and counsel sweet as from the lips of a beloved consort. – *Kāvyaprakāśa* 1.2

First four purposes are for the poet; the last two for the reader/viewer. Mammaṭa in his commentary on this verse first gives examples of how these purposes are achieved, and then adds:

> The chief aim of *kāvya*, however, is the attainment of the pure unmixed pleasure that follows instantaneously on the experiencing of *rasa*. When [*kāvya*] exercises its full functions, it helps the development of various *rasas*, sublating the direct effect of the word and its meaning. As such poetry differs from the Vedas, in which the word, in the form of a master's command, predominates; it differs also from the Purāṇas, in which the predominant element is the friendly counsel [not to be followed literally]. Such [*kāvya*] is the work of [*kavis*], clever in depicting things in a manner passing the comprehension of ordinary men; it offers to other poets and cultured men counsel most persuasively, like a beloved wife, by means of a moving tenderness in the manner of it [that is, in the words] – counsel such as that one should behave like Rāma and not Rāvaṇa and as such [*kāvya*] is by all means to be studied and cultivated.
>
> – *Kāvyaprakāśa*, chapter 1

Viśvanātha uses the term *phala* (fruit) and not *prayojana* (purpose), which suggests that no one composes *kāvya* with an express design – a good *kāvya*, by its very nature, has the desired effects or fruit. With this substitution, Viśvanātha shifts the perspective from the poet/composer to the hearer/reader. He says that through *kāvya* even those with limited intelligence can attain the four ends of life. The four ends of life are a part of the Indian world-view (*darśana*). Man's life is for the fulfilment of these four ends – *dharma, artha, kāma* and *mokṣa*. One who destroys these, destroys everything. One who saves these, saves everything. These four ends of life relate to four different levels – at the level of philosophy (individual's ultimate goal), the purpose is *mukti* (liberation from the self); at the level of the worldly, social life, the purpose is *dharma* (right conduct); at the level of individual worldly pursuits, the purpose is *artha* (wealth and other means); and at the psychic level, it is *kāma* (the satisfaction of desires and fulfilment of wishes). *Kāvya* helps attain these *puruṣārthas* for, as Kuntaka says, Śāstra eradicates *avidyā, kāvya* eradicates *aviveka* (lack of discrimination).

Though the four ends of life are invoked as part of the total conceptual system, the classical tradition holds fast to the attainment of pure happiness (*ānanda*) coincident with *rasa* as the primary goal of poetry. With later theorists (Abhinavagupta, etc.), this *ānanda* becomes a transcendental experience, something closer to *paramānanda* (happiness in the liberation of the self through identity with the larger Self) than *viṣayānanda* (pleasure of indulgence in objects of senses). As in every other area of thought, in the definition of the effect of literary experience also, there is a movement from the mundane to the divine, physical to metaphysical. What remains constant is the claim that in *kāvya, ānanda* is the means of attainment of the four ends of life. As Viśvanātha says:

> Through Vedas and Śāstras, the four ends are attained without *rasa* and with lot of *duḥkha* (suffering) and are possible only for one who has a mature mind. But as *kāvya* is the product of *ānandasamūha* (aggregate of pleasures), it helps even young immature minds to attain the four ends.
>
> – *Sāhitya-Darpaṇa*, chapter 1

Role of Literature in Society

The question of what role the literary discourse has *vis-à-vis* other discourses in the given society is pertinent only in societies, such as India's, that have attested traditions of thought in diverse domains of knowledge. Where, as in India, we have Dharmaśāstras, Arthaśāstras, Kāmaśāstras and Mokṣaśāstras (for the realization of the acknowledged four ends of life), it was pointedly asked what is the exact role of literature when we have texts for all the main goals of life. The answer is that literature functions as *dṛṣṭānta* for all the four knowledge traditions, i.e. through constructed narratives, it exemplifies the ideas in the life, actions and events of recognizable individuals.

Literature and Life: As Mimetic Art

The discussion of literature as a mimetic art goes back to Plato's definition of all art as "imitation", a representation and therefore less than "real". He went on to analyse the nature of representation, the "image" and distinguished "appearance" and "being". Aristotle distinguished three modes of representation: (1) of things as they are, (2) of things as they appear to be, and (3) of things as they ought to be. This is relatable to such modes of representation as "surrealism", "realism" and "idealism". The substantial questions are the nature of representation and the relationship of literary enactment to life. The critic examines the total reality of object (what is the total reality of an object?) and its recreation in language.

In *Republic* Bk. X, we have Plato's theory of mimesis, of all art (including literature) as imitation of reality. This is a continuation of the discussion of reality in the two famous images – "the line image" and "the cave image" (Bks. VI and VII). We have already been told that the visible, tangible forms are but "images" of the ultimate idea, and we have also been told that "images" are not exact reproductions – they deviate from what they are images of more or less. The art-objects (painting, sculpture, poem, character in a narrative, an event in a tragedy, etc.) are but "images" – tangible, visible manifestations of the real. We posit a single idea for various multiplicities – "the idea of a couch" for so many diverse couches. The craftsman, when he makes a couch, makes something resemble the idea of a couch he has in his mind – an imitation.

For surely no craftsman makes the idea itself. It is like reflecting something in a mirror. What the artists "create" or "craft" is:

> . . . the appearance of them, but not the reality . . . only a dim adumbration in comparison with reality.

God is "the real author of the couch that has a real being . . ." and the carpenter is the "maker" of the couch. The painter who paints the couch is an "imitator",

> the producer of the product three removes from nature, you call imitator.

And this applies "to the maker of tragedies" also. There is the "truth"; then "phantasm" (object); then "imitation of the phantasm" – mimetic art therefore is far removed from truth.

One can produce imitations "without knowledge of the truth" and it is because Homer is only an imitator and speaks of "wars and generalship and the administration of cities and the education of men" without any real knowledge of these things that he has not influenced any city or life for the better.

> What city credits you . . . having benefited them?

asks Socrates.

All the poetic tribes are "imitators of images of excellence . . . and do not lay hold on truth . . ." and the readers/hearers are likely to be misled, particularly those "who see things only through words". So literature can create a misleading illusion of reality:

> The imitator knows nothing worth mentioning of the things he imitates, but that imitation is a form of play, not to be taken seriously. . . .

This is a serious indictment of poetry (literature) as a valid means of knowledge.

In fact, literature/poetry can have a deleterious effect – it appeals to the inferior (and not nobly serious) part of the mind, the emotions:

> . . . for it waters and fosters these feelings when what we aught to do is to dry them up.

Emotions are not to be indulged in, and "a good and reasonable man" shall

> keep quiet as far as possible in calamity and not (to) chafe and repine . . .

Literature (poetry) "waters" the emotions and weakens reason and self-control. So poets shall not be allowed in our city:

> for if you grant admission to the honeyed Muse in lyric or epic, pleasure and pain will be lords of your city instead of law . . .

There is an ancient enmity (opposition), says Plato between philosophy and poetry, and between the two, philosophy (Socrates) is the instrument of truth, "not" poetry (Homer). However, if it can be shown that poetry (literature) has a place in "a well-governed state", in civilised human affairs, "we would gladly admit her (poetry)". Plato, therefore invites.

> all her advocates . . . "not poets but lovers of poetry" to plead her cause in prose without metre (that is in a reasoned discourse) . . . and show that she (poetry) is not only

> delightful but beneficial to orderly government and all the/ life of man.

This invitation to defend poetry has been taken seriously in the Western tradition. Aristotle's poetics is itself such a defence and we have already mentioned Tacitus' defence. In the English tradition itself, Sidney and Shelley composed their famous defences ('apologies').

The Indian tradition has not been remiss in the discussion of reality and its representation as verbal images. All art, including the verbal art, is image-making – the making of images that have a given relationship to what they are images of: chair made by a carpenter is only an image, a representation, of the form that the carpenter had in his mind. So is the shadow of a tree an image of the tree, the reflection in the mirror, an image of my face, the idol of a feeling, an idea or a fact. In the other cosmic sense this vast, visible, multiple, diverse physical world is treated in certain schools of thoughts as a mere image of the real. The whole world is either full of only images or is itself an image. One way, this cognizable universe is a "successive series" of images, as in Plato's ontology (vide, *Republic*) where in the visible world is a complex of images that are images of other images and so on till you reach the level of ideational essence and the universe is thus a structure of varying degrees of illusion (phantasm). The other way, in Vedānta, this whole cognizable universe is a continuous chain of images, all of them together being merely diverse forms of the Ultimate Real.

What are these images? What is it an image of? What is the nature of an image/representation? What creative process is involved in image? What is the goal of imaging? And finally what is the role of the images, the artist and his relation to the reality he seeks to represent? This structure of images, a whole theory of representation, is implicit in Socrates' positing of the carpenter as the paradigm artist (*Republic*, Bk. X), a maker of not "the real being but something that resembles real being". For Socrates, God is the true creator, "the true and natural begetter" of just "one couch in nature" that possesses the ultimate "form or idea". This couch has "real being", is "in nature unique" but by virtue of its possessing a form is already one – remove from the essence. The carpenter is also a maker but "he does not make the idea or form which we say is the real couch, the couch in itself, but only some *particular* couch" (italics mine). Being "in the complete sense" does not belong to the work of the carpenter (or to that of any handicraftsman) but nevertheless, he is a creator, a maker of a relatively valid representation which is only twice removed from "the truth" – the chair he makes is "an imitation of reality as it is . . . of the thing in itself in nature". The painter on the other hand, is an "imitiator". So is the poet, "the maker of tragedies", also an imitator, "in his nature three removes from the thing and the truth". The poet or the painter imitates not the reality of things, but their appearance, the "phantasm" not "the truth" but the object as it is cognized by him, as it figures in his mind. Thus his representation, "lays hold of only a small part of the object" and is directed at "appearance as it appears".

A whole theory of reality and its representation are implicit in this Greek paradigm of the carpenter. A fourfold ontology is postulated – levels of the real, of existence, of image, of illusion (phantom). The artist is a creator or maker of images – he is the master of his material; he measures it, cuts it, segments it and rearranges it to produce a form – it is an analogue of the Greek geometry-centred conception of reality as space, as quantifiable measurement. He actually "produces" a form out of this, brings a "form" into being. This form is an analogue of the ultimate but is not the ultimate – there is a gap, a falling off between the ultimate and its representation. Though not possessed of the "complete" being, it yet participates in the real.

Now the paradigm artist/craftsman in the Indian tradition is *kumbhakāra* (the potter). Implicit, in this choice of a different paradigm is a different conception of reality and its representation. The potter attaches his hands to the clay rotating on the wheel, shuts his eyes, and waits for the immanent form in the clay and the form he saw in his mind to become one. He does not quantify or measure, nor segment nor does he rearrange his material. The reality in this paradigm is not quantifiable, not measurable, not segmentable and is not amenable to reordering or rearrangement – 'reality' is an ocean, says the *Ṛgveda* (I.164.45). Nor does the potter create a form; he does not bring a form into being – he merely helps a form to manifest itself, a form that was always there, that is inherent in the clay, along with other forms, a form that he as one endowed with a special perception (*krāntādarśinaḥ*) has actually seen in his mind. His mind, his body and the clay become a continuity and his hands feel the manifestation of the form – one may say the form flows from his mind through his hands to merge with, become one with, the form in the clay. The visible form that becomes manifest is a representation, an image, of the form in the clay – for the form in the clay continues to be there – even when the visible form has taken shape, for, notice that the potter may collapse this particular realization and once again make the form manifest itself in another visible form.

Theory of Images

This manifest form we said is an image, a representation. What is its relationship to the immanent form then – the being of this form? Is it the same as the real form? It is the same, yet it is not the same – the potter would always say he hasn't been able to make visible what he really saw, yet it cannot be said that it is something as a potential in the clay. The real form is in this visible form; and yet it is not in this visible form. This is the mystery and one that is familiar to the students of that school of Indian philosophical thinking that finally evolved into Advaita, the non-dualist world-view.

This manifest form is a representation, an image. What is its relationship to what it is an image of? Consider the fact that the potter does not "do" something; he does not "make" something – he is not a *kartā* (the agent). In true conformity with the Indian world-view, he is only an instrument, a *kāraṇa*, not even a *karaṇa*, for *karaṇa* is the clay. In the conjunction of the potter, the wheel and the clay, a form happens to manifest itself. What is this process of manifestation? Five sets of trans-disciplinary constructs articulate the conceptual universe of this process:

i. *amūrtta*	*mūrtta*	unembodied formless	embodied/with form
ii. *avyakta*	*vyakta*	non-manifest	manifest
iii. *dravya*	*rūpa/ākr̥ti*	substance	particular shape within the ken of senses
iv. *dharmī*	*dharma*	substratum inseparable property attribute	inseparable property/attribute
v. *kāraṇa*	*kārya*	cause	effect/action

Two kinds of interrelated cognizable, ontological entities are posited by each of these five sets. It is wrong to talk of "levels" in this world-view; what one can say is that the paired constructs belong to two modes of being. Both the two modes are cognitively real and simultaneously coexisting: one of them is conceptual inferred and ineffable from the other which has a sensory reality (the mind also being one of the senses). The sensory mode helps construct the abstract. The image or representation belongs to the sensory mode. For what the potter instruments is an embodiment, a manifest form, a property or a particular shape effect. As the wheel turns, the *amūrtta* also manifests as *mūrtta*, the *avyakta* (*sattā*) as *vyakta* (*sattva*) the *dharmi* as *dharma*, the *dravya* as *rūpa*, and thus the two modes, though separately continuing to be real, seem to merge into one.

The *kumbhakāra*'s creativity modulates one mode of reality into another – *dravya* into *rūpa* etc. (without, of course, the destruction of *dravya* which alone is indestructible). Similarly, when the poet puts an experience/emotion into words, the experience continues to exist independent of the words and yet it appears inseparable from words.

The second mode – *pratibimba* (counter-image) – brings as we said, the first mode – itself a *bimba* (image) (of the ultimate undifferentiated *sattā*) – within the realm of sensory cognition. In a remarkable couplet, Sant Kabīr has explained, once and for all the function of the image (counter image), the relation that holds between the image and the object imaged. He says when an image is seen in a mirror, the same one embodied observer appears to be present both inside the mirror and outside. That is, in the same one person, two attributes – a counter image and an image postulated on the basis of the counter image – become perceptible; or one may say that on account of the postulated counter image, the same one object appears in two forms. That is, in the absence of the conditional/causal factors (*upādhi*) – the mirror in this case – only one is perceptible. The counter image makes possible the cognition of the object (image). The function therefore of the image is to make manifest the *tattva bhāva* of an object and to instrument just that kind of an image is the end or goal of an artist/craftsman. What is the *tattva/bhāva* of an object that the artist is instrumental in making manifest. It is, therefore, the function of the image to make manifest, one could say construct, the object – it constructs it by imaging its essence, the *tattva* or *bhāva*. The objects are *saṅketas* (indicators or signs) of the real – these forms do not belong to reality and yet they appear as one with it. These objects themselves are *bimba* (image) of the ultimate, and are themselves in turn imaged in art and discourse. In themselves they are complex realities, almost inexpressible through representations, for the totality of an object is a complex matrix of a number of categories. One may begin with the Jain assertion eschewing the dogmatic view, that an object is *anantadharmātmaka* (has endless properties):

> All things (*vastus*) thus possess an infinite number of qualities each of which can only be affirmed in a particular sense. Such an ordinary thing as a jug will be found to be the object of an infinite number of affirmations and the possessor of an infinite number of qualities from infinite points of view. . . .
>
> – S.N. Dasgupta, *A History of Indian Philosophy*, vol. I, p. 176

Complete knowledge of an object involves a deep awareness of how, to what degree and in what manner, these categories/ attributes have been realized in that particular object and an artist can "image" an object only when he has grasped its totality. But how does one gain such full knowledge of an object? Mental mediation or intellection is necessary to grasp accurately even a perceived object. It is argued:

> The primary thing has no form till it is determined by the mind. – *VP* III.14.350

The Yoga system distinguishes three dimensions of an object – (i) *nāma* (its designation), (ii) *rūpa* (its form or appearance), and (iii) *jñāna* (knowledge) that arises from its verbal designation. The object *ghaṭa* is different from all the three – the word *ghaṭa* is different from the earthen object it denotes;

its form (*rūpa*) that we perceive is only a small part of the reality of *ghaṭa* and not separable from its substance; the object which is cognized when we hear the word *ghaṭa* is a conception of our *citta* (the consciousness) and therefore different from the object *ghaṭa* and is asymmetrical with the existential reality of the object.

How is its knowledge gained? How is the object constituted in our consciousness? To be able to do so, the mind with reverence to the object that the artist wishes to represent. The artist/craftsman in the Indian thought has to be a *yogī*, a *sādhaka* and a *mantrin* – a *yogī* because he yokes his mind to the object, a *sādhaka* because he is a devotee full of reverence or love, and a *mantrin* because he reflects and cogitates. Different stages in this creative process, this *yoga-sādhanā*, have been explicitly described in the Buddhist thought. The artist begins by a ceremonial purification of his self, and both the mind and the body are purified. He then withdraws into solitude to enable himself to focus on the object of his meditation. In the third stage, he performs daily acts of worship to cultivate love and reverence. Then he consciously inculcates the four "infinite moods" – of friendliness, compassion, sympathy and impartiality. He then meditates on *śūnyatā* (the great void) to destroy his pride. At that state, he begins to meditate on the essence and, finally, he meditates on the form of the object. His oneness with the object, now is such that the object virtually materializes itself before him and all that he has to do now is to transcribe it. The theory claims that the entire "image" – the idol, the poem, the picture is visualized and composed as a whole in the mind before it is actually transferred onto the page, before it is transcribed.

What is the nature of the image that gets constituted in the transcription. Since the image manifests an object as it figures in the mind, it may not bear much palpable resemblance to the object it is an image of. It may only evoke a remembrance generally resembling the experience of the object. It could also be an image of something that has no real existence or, an image could represent only a part of the reality of an object; or, conversely, it could represent more than the reality of an object and even when it faithfully represents an object, it is still only a partial representation because it does not share its spatial and temporal co-ordinates and it has no content unlike the object it represents.

Bhartṛhari, while discussing verbal representation of objects, dwells on those properties of an image through several examples. An image may thus be a mere resemblance on the basis of appearance of objects – mirage resembles water but in spite of the similarity, mirage is not water (*VP* II.287). An image may evoke a cognition similar to that of the original though again, it does not have the functional properties of the original:

> Even though one sees ups and downs in a picture, similar to those of mountains, still it does not cause obstruction. . . .
> – *VP* II.290

Again, apart from all these, an image may not share the proportions of the individual:

> Mountains and other well-known objects cover a wide area but their reflection covers only a small area. – *VP* II.294

Again the image may have no real existence and is more or less like something seen in a dream:

> While real poison and other such things are the causes of death, the same things seen in a dream are not capable of causing the same.

Again an image may represent some thing more than the original – for example, a painted blue sky may be more blue than it could actually ever be. Again an image would always be partial – in a painting, it remains a one-sided view of the object painted – and, finally, an image may in fact be quite contrary to the real – the hundred-headed Śeṣanāga, for example, or the idols of Lord Gaṇeśa.

An image may therefore be less or more than the object, deviant in proportion, unreal, counter-factual and/or partial in the expression of the objects' attributes or be devoid of them altogether – but, and this is important, it is designed to be non-perceptible essence (*bhāva*) of the object which is expressible only through such a constructed image. This image constructed by the object, in turn constructs the object for the auditors.

In the West, Plato, at the beginning of the tradition referred to the image-making as a mimetic art "far removed from truth" (*Republic*, Bk. X) and inquired into the status of an image of a portrait, of a sculpture, or of a verbal representation. What is the relationship between an image and what it is an image of? Does an image capture the entire reality? In its perfect analogue? No, says, Plato:

> I should say rather that the image, if expressing in every point the entire reality, would no longer be an image.
>
> – *Cratylus*

Images have some other "principles of truth" and are images only when "something is added or subtracted" (*Cratylus*). In *Sophist*, he had divided the art of image-making into "the making of likenesses (icon) . . . creating a copy that conforms to the proportion of the original" and what may be called a "semblance" (fantasma). Creating a copy on the other hand that conforms to the properties of the original is likeness. Such likeness, fidelity, in some images – colossal statues, for example – creates a distortion in appearance and the upper part appears disproportionately smaller. So the artist, Phidias the sculptor, made the upper part that much proportionately longer so that by the introduction of that deviation, untruth, the statue appears 'true' or real:

> This is creating semblance. In the first, the proportions (of being) are true, but the image appears false; in the other, the proportions (of being) are false, but image seems true. This is the great anomaly of representation in art.
>
> This semblance or *fantasia* that the artist creates is a class that baffles. . . . This "appearing" or "seeming" and the saying of something which yet is not true – falsehoods have a real existence. – *Sophist*

These principles of imaging have implications for literature. Ordinary language itself is intrinsically imagistic – sharing in the properties of images. For example, there is no "dewy wine" and birds are not "immortal" – but these apparently false cognitions capture forms of reality that would otherwise escape representation. Even a *svabhāvokti* (an ordinary utterance) like "cat!" would evoke/suggest widely disparate mental pictures to the listeners. Words are signs, says Bhartṛhari, of the images or reflections that are cast on our intellect (*citta*):

> That which is projected on the insentient (*acetana*) forms of the intellect (*citta*) as a reflection (*pratibimba*), it is that which is the basis of the use of words. – *VP* III.14.325

Verbal Image — Meaning in Literature

Like all images, verbal image is also partial. Verbal communication relates "only to a part of an aspect of reality, or to the determination of the intended object by an external factor, or to a reversal of reality, or to an absence of it" (*VP* III.3.52).

For example:

1. The *pot* broke (there is no reference to the "colour" of the pot)
2. The *ear-rings* shine (not ear-rings – "gold" of which they are made)

3. The *horned-rabbit* (there is no "horned" rabbit in real life)
4. The *sky is above us* (there is no "sky" as such).

So in verbal usage, says Bhartṛhari, there is another being, a secondary being that is different from the external, perceptible being–

> When words convey the objects the things so conveyed have a Being distinct from their external Being. It consists in their figuring in the mind. . . .

The mind can conceive objects which have no external Being and the words convey them as they are conceived in the mind:

> "fire-circle" (*alāta-cakra*) and "rabbit-horns" (*śaśa viṣāna*). In verbal usage it is the secondary Being that is involved.
>
> – *Vṛtti* on III.3.39

This involvement of secondary Being is exemplified in negation as well – "not happy" is a reflex of a unitary, positive secondary Being in the speaker's mind. The existence of primary objects is not denied; all that is being claimed is that in language, the objects, both existent and non-existent, are talked about in terms of their secondary Being.

Words denote only a part of the object. A particular property or feature of the object is not a part of the meaning of a word – the word "table" does not incorporate the meaning of its height or length. The material of which the object is constituted is also not part of the meaning of a word – that the "table" is made of marble or wood is not part of its denotation. Similarly the properties (*guṇa*s) are not part of the meaning of a word though some of them may be necessarily understood – so qualities have to be specifically expressed by separate words – "blue sky", for example "in qualities like white, though present (in the rice) are not meant to be conveyed by the word rice . . ." (*VP* II.69). Again the form of the object is not a part of the meaning:

> An expressive word (like *ghata* = a jar) does not denote the shapes and forms of a jar as it rests only on the general idea (that is common to all the jars). – *VP* II.123

Kriyās (functions) of an object are also not denoted – nor does the word denote *avasthā, lakṣaṇa, deśa, kliṣṭa–akliṣṭa* or class.

As against this intrinsic partial denotation, there is the excess of denotation in the evocation of associated, secondary and figurative meanings besides the primary meaning. For example, in the names of flowers – e.g. *rose* – the qualities associated with the smell are often understood but they are not invariably present in the object. "Cognitions of hearers take place which are qualified by all the associated things" (*VP* III.14.473). Example is given of the word *brāhmaṇa* which is invariably associated with certain acts and which is understood through convention to possess certain qualities (*VP* III.14.481). The word *putra* (son) is qualified by actions which are associated with it in the world (*VP* III.14.508). And the adjective "black" may be applied to an object even when only a part of the object is black (*VP* III.406). In the same way words also have, or acquire, a secondary or extended meaning on the basis of a cognizable resemblance – for example, the use of the word *parvata* for a reflection of the mountain in water and of *ghoṛā* for a clay horse. Bhartṛhari explains the basis of such extensions:

> Just as a lamp reveals, in an object like a jar, through association (or proximity) other things than that for the illumination of which it was employed.
>
> In the same way, a word conveys, from among the things which are connected together those that are different from one to convey which it was used. – *VP* II.298-99

Sometimes the meanings so evoked are unintended – just as fire produces unintended smoke:

> In the same way, a word also, when a particular meaning is meant to be conveyed, denotes by association, an unintended meaning also.
>
> Just as one cannot abandon (while taking a thing) something which is very closely connected with it, in the same way a word cannot but denote what is intimately connected with its primary meaning. – *VP* II.301-02

When the boundaries of denotation are so fluid, the focus on some one aspect of meaning is brought about by the speaker's *vivakṣā* (intention) and the hearer in order to grasp the intended meaning has to reconstruct the speaker's intention. The same object may be presented differently by different speakers or even by the same speaker on the two different occasions – thus one may use the word horse to denote its endurance or its speed or its proportionate beauty. In the same way the speaker may "reorder" reality in his representation or expression of that reality, something which is a quality of mental images and is often present in paintings.

> Sometimes objects which are far from one another are presented as being connected and those which are near one another are presented as being apart.
>
> Separation of what is united and union of what is separated; what are many are presented as one and what is one as many. – *VP* II.431-32

There is thus great variety and lack of fixity in the way objects are expressed by words. Thus the word "water" may refer to a "drop" or "ocean" (*VP* II.156), depending on what "is fashioned by the mind" (*VP* II.3.88). The form of an object is determined by one's memory or experience of the object. In fact, when a word is used, "a rememberance resembling the experience of the object" figures in the mind of the speaker and also takes place in the hearer's mind (*VP* II.417).

Since each speaker and each hearer brings his own "rememberance", there is great relativism in verbal denotation both in comprehension and expression. This has been stated in four *kārikās*:

> Just as our sense perceive the same object in different ways, in the same way, an object is understood from words in different ways. – *VP* II.134
>
> The meaning of words, intended by the speaker to be one thing, is understood by different listeners differently, according to their own background. – *VP* II.135
>
> With regard to the same thing, one's views undergo change. The same person sees the same thing differently. – *VP* II.136
>
> To one and the same word are attributed many meanings by one and the same person or by many persons according to undefined circumstances. – *VP* II.137

In the sense that the "meaning" has to be determined through intellection, in the process of communication, the words are based in the speaker's cognition and they are interpreted in the hearer's mind.

Whole sentences too are propositional images and the role of mental mediation in the determination of their meaning is equally clear. They have to be interpreted in the light of a large number of factors of internal and external contexts, such as situation, propriety, place, time, connection, separation, association, opposition, context, indication, the presence of another word, suitability, gender and intonation. (see *VP* II.314-16). Thus:

> An enlightened hearer knows that praise and blame, meant to promote action and abstention from action respectively, are really unreal.
>
> Even if sometimes, the truth is told in connection with praise or blame, the object is always to teach action or abstention

> from action. – *VP* II.319, 24

Hence, great care and thought are needed to determine the meaning of words in a text. The listener (or reader), once hearing understood the meaning of words separately, has

> a flash of understanding . . . which they call the meaning of the sentence, brought about by the meaning of the individual words. – *VP* II.143

This sentential meaning, this one individuals' amalgamation, is indefinable (*avicārita*) (II.145). Hence the need for exposition, exegesis and explanation, yet the impossibility of wholly communicating it – it cannot be explained to others as such and such:

> *It is experienced by everyone within himself* and even the subject (of the experience) is not able to render an account of it to himself. – *VP* II.144

As we have explained elsewhere (see K. Kapoor, "Concept of Padārtha in Language and Philosophy" *William Jones Commemorative Volume,* Deccan College, Pune, 1994), when we observe an object ("jar" in this case), our pre-existing knowledge is brought up to our consciousness – it is only a reflection because the knowledge continues to exist in our self even after it is brought up and impressed on our consciousness – we say image of the external object because the total reality of the external object is not grasped and projected on to our consciousness but only our particular perception of the object. This interaction produces an understanding, in the mind, a mental image and this object "figuring in the mind" is the basis of word usage. Our knowing self, and the knowledge in our self is a sequenceless unity but when it comes in contact with different external objects and attaches to them, we become aware of a diversified, fragmented consciousness which otherwise "has no diversity of form of its own" (*VP* III.14.324). A distinction between the ontological object "X" and our knowledge or consciousness of this object, "this is X" has to be maintained. The "X" in the latter is a mental construct, asymmetrical with its ontological analogue:

All worldly usage, Bhartṛhari says,

> is carried out with objects created by mental construction.
> – *VP* III.3.82

And again –

> The primary thing has no form till it is determined by the mind. – *VP* III.14.350

It is this sense of creating the cognition of *ghaṭa–paṭa bheda* that language cuts forms in the ocean of reality. This is Bhartṛhari's theory of reality being a linguistic (mental) construct. It is clear that whether we look upon Bhartṛhari's theory of meaning as an epistemology for the structure of reality or as an ontology that describes the structure of meaning in language, it is a theory that is the underpinning of transcendental doctrines (in both reality and language), predicates the mental or conceptual reality of even physical or external objects and depends heavily, therefore, on such processes of mental mediation as generalization, inference, reduction and metaphoricization. Only thus understood, can the complex universe of meaning be organized into a structure.

Literary language is all the more figural – images are pervasive and consciously employed to constitute meaning. This fantasma of literary representation is required so that "the realm of pure feeling can find utterance" (Cassirer, *Language and Myth*, p. 99) or else "what could we know of the innumerable nuances in the aspects of things". As another modern philosopher of symbolic form has noted, there is an approach to some final truth and reality through understanding "the symbolic forms of language". The verbal image is the way in which the ideational content of an object is apprehended and expressed. Taking Keats' *Ode to a Nightingale* as an example, one can cite a number of images that are shifted analogues of what they represent, conceptual constructs to connote the nuances and the fullness of experience. The Indian thinkers call it *bhāva abhivyakti* (expression of the real being). One is able to construct the "truth" of the object/experience represented from these shifted representations. There is a piece of land that is "melodious" and there is a kind of mirth that is "sunburnt" and what kind of going-away is "fade away" of Keats? What are "murmurous haunts" and what is "verdurous gloom"? And how is a bird "immortal"? And what is "embalmed darkness"? We awaken to newer shades of experience as we work out these images. In that manner the changing intensity of the sunshine in the bubbles becomes "winking" and cool, clear wine becomes "dewy".

One may also note the juxtaposition and foregrounding of certain images to create patterns or densities of meaning – the repetition of "sad", "fade" and "forlorn", and the idea of "darkness" to foreground the central heartache and the recurrent opposition of "darkness" and "light" is there to underscore the simultaneity of joys and sorrows – only that the "light" merely intersperses the pervasive gloom and then, too, through divine grace. Read as such, the poem is a highly inflected statement of the state of the self with complex cognitions figurally represented in an asymmetrical language to make manifest the *bhāva* (being) of the poet's experience.

The *alaṁkārika* (figural mode) is the characteristic that separates literary discourse from other rational discourses. Even otherwise ordinary language as a constructivist system constitutes a world that is a shifted representation of the real. And language, on account of its discreteness and sequentiality, is intrinsically asymmetrical with reality. This being so, how reliable is the knowledge embodied in literature and what is the status of literature as a discourse of knowledge?

Status of Literature as a Discourse of Knowledge

Both in the East and West, there is a long history of debate about the status of literature as a discourse of knowledge, about its value and validity as a rational discourse. This debate stems from the very nature of literature as an art form, one that makes copies of the real, gives a form to what is formless, makes an idol out of an idea.

We have noted that all art is representation, the making of images. The desirability or otherwise of making images, determined as it is by what epistemological validity is assigned to them, has been a major cultural divide between the Semitic and the Aryan civilizations. At the source of the Western tradition, Plato, in his ontology of a reality graded from the gross, visible level of "shadows" to the subtle, intelligible level of ideas, used the term "image" for a representation, divided all images into "likenesses" and "semblances" and considered all of them as "corruptions of the mind". In Indian thought, we conceptualize an image as *mūrti* and call the artist, *mūrtikāra* (one who gives a visible form). *Mūrti* is a "concrete shape" in the world of senses, a (sensible) form of what is essentially formless. Though it can be possessed of all the powers of the original – through *prāṇa-pratiṣṭhā* – it remains, nevertheless, a *pratibimba* (a reflection, a shadow).

Aristotle explains that imaging is a mode of constituting knowledge: the desire to imitate, to make images, he says is innate to human nature because imitation has something to do with learning about the world, with our knowledge of the world – we delight in imitation because we are learning all the time:

> Imitation is natural to man . . . it is also natural for all to delight in works of imitation. . . . The truth of this second point is shown by experience: though the objects themselves may be painful to see, we delight to view the most realistic representations of them in art. . . . The explanation is to be found in a further fact: to be learning something is the greatest of pleasures not only to the philosopher but also to the rest of mankind . . . the reason of the delight . . . is . . . that one is at the same time learning – gathering the meaning of things . . .
>
> – *Poetics* 4

In the Western tradition then, the motivation for representation is the "delight" in imitation is in the enlargement of learning, in the increase in knowledge that accompanies both the creation as well as the enjoyment of a representation. Our own thinking has some affinity with this. Bharata uses the term *anukaraṇa* (second doing), a reconstruction, an enactment – there is an experience and that experience is re-enacted out of, and away from, its original totality of time, place, agency, etc. On the other hand, a sense of instrumentality is codified in the term that *Nāṭyaśāstra* uses for a representation *abhinaya,* which literally means "that which is the path to/guides or leads to the knowledge of the real".

And as *Rasagaṅgādhara* says representation is a source of joy (*ānanda*) both to the performer/maker and the auditor and this comes from a complete inwardness with, a complete knowledge of what the *mūrti* (the image) represents – *mūrti* makes manifest, *vyakta*, embodies, what is non-manifest, *avyakta*. The *avyakta* category is quite complex – an actually existing object in the external world is very much manifest at one level but it is not manifest in its totality and a large part of its being is beyond perception. That is how and why a painter can make us see the object that we have looked at often but never experienced the way we experience it in its visual image. This is more true of the inner realities – the mental conceptions and the feelings of the heart which a poet alone can make real for us in his verbal images. Another set of related terms from Indian thought articulates the concept of *mūrti* as "an investment of what is without form (*amūrtta*) with the visibility/comprehensibility/sensibility of a form". A representation thus by making manifest what is unmanifest and making sensible what is beyond perception makes possible our cognition of the totality of an object. This totality as constituted in the work of art is the totality as experienced by the poet or the painter or the potter. In this sense, it is an *abhivyakti* an effort to manifest something, to bring something into being. As such, literary or art statement is an individual's statement and contingent for its truth on the individual consciousness.

Now cultures differ, have differed, about this process of imaging, of embodying an idea, of giving a body to an idea of the real, in short, the desirability of making images, of cognizing an idea as idea or cognizing the idea as an idol. For the semitic, monotheistic systems, the idea of the real must exist only at the formless, disembodied ideational level. To make an idol, an image, of the idea is to create an illusion, a fiction, a falsehood which is deleterious for the morals of man. This point of view has off and on been an equally important principle of such reformist systems of thought in India as early Buddhism and early Sikhism. In the Semitic world-view, to return to our theme, to make a copy of a part of the concrete world which is real, physically real, and which has been created as such by One Almighty God is, blasphemous and presumptuous. Make no images, said Moses:

> You saw no form of any kind the day the Lord spoke to you.
>
> . . .
>
> Therefore watch yourself very carefully, so that you do not make for yourself an idol, an image of any shape. . . ."
>
> – Deuteronomy 4:15-16

Giving a form, a significant shape, to an abstraction, such as God, is a corruption of the original, and, besides, in Semitic theology:

> . . . beware lest you act coruptly by making a graven image for yourselves . . . – Deuteronomy 4:17

This uncompromising monotheistic principle of abstraction alone being real – a theological and pragmatic response to the Jewish history of pendulum swings between divisive polytheism and a monotheism unifying in its effect – is in opposition to its archetypal adversary, the Hellenist/Aryan principle of plurality of gods, of polytheism. The Semitic principle denies validity to the psychic freedom to conceptualize, and to render, in a desired and a desirable form (*sākāra*) with given attributes (*saguṇa*) what is necessarily recognized as essentially formless (*nirākāra*) and attributeless (*nirguṇa*). While the Jews have remained uncompromising *nirguṇavādīs*, Christianity satisfied this psychic and cognitive need to "see", to "visualize" by imaging the Son of God – Christ on the cross, Christ in Nativity, Christ at Last Supper – and the angels. Islam turned calligraphy into a visual art to satisfy the same psychic need. It is to be remembered that the ancient Semitic no-images world was surrounded by the image-making Greeks – and thus the two antagonistic principles existed cheek by jowl for centuries. This contiguity of the other model explains the historic Jewish deviations into Hellenisms. It also explains Plato's conception of the ideational essence as the ultimate real, the visible being only a shadow or an image (*Republic* VI). Isn't Socrates arguing the Greek view and ascribing a certain incompleteness to the Semitic world-view? And yet, the reality of the visible is just that much suspect in Socrates suggesting an influence of the Semitic thought.

In fact, in a language strangely close to that of Deuteronomy, Socrates says about the verbal images:

> . . . you will not betray me to the tragic poets and all other

> imitators – that kind of art seems to be a corruption of the mind . . . – *Republic*, Bk. X

On the one hand, we have a world-view in which only the abstract, the ideational is real and its image, therefore, is necessarily a falsehood, a phantom and therefore misleading. On the other hand, a continuity is visualized from the abstract to the concrete, from the conceptual to the actual. Since all literature is verbal image-making, a stand on this ontological difference would determine its validity and value as a discourse of knowledge. For Plato, therefore, for whom "mimetic art is far removed from truth" and verbal images are "three removes from nature (reality)" (*Republic*, Bk. X), literature is not a valid means of knowledge. In a serious indictment, Plato says:

> All the poetic tribes are imitators of images . . . and do not lay hold on truth . . . mimetic art is far removed from truth . . . it touches or lays hold of only a small part of the object and that a phantom. – *Republic*, Bk. X

And this can mislead readers/auditors, particularly those "who see things only through words". Its source of creativity being inspiration which is akin to madness, its appeal is not to the rational self but to the lawer emotional self:

> . . . for it waters and fosters those feelings when what we aught to do is to dry them up. – *Republic*, Bk. X

Poets do not create *with* knowledge, for literary compositions are, ". . . easy to produce without knowledge of the truth" and that the poets know nothing worth mentioning of the things they write about and that their work is:

> a form of play not to be taken seriously . . . for it is phantoms, not realities, that they produce. – *Republic*, Bk. X

More than the ontological and epistemological objection to literary representation, Plato objects while talking of Homer, "its leader", to its doubtful ethical value and emotional effect – the spectacle of unrestrained emotion is morally damaging. In sum, literature can lay no claim to being a rational discourse, to being a statement of knowledge. The reliable means of knowledge for Plato is then not Homer but Socrates.

It has been pointed out that in the Bk. X of the *Republic,*

> when Plato has completed his final burning denunciation of poetry, the false siren, the imitator of things which are themselves shadows, the ally of all that is low and weak . . .

he adds with a touch of compunction:

> we will give her champions, not poets themselves but poet-lovers, an opportunity to make her defence. . . .

Aristotle certainly knew the passage, and it looks as if his treatise on poetry was the first response to Plato's challenge. (Gilbert Murray, Introduction to Byford's edition of Aristotle's *Poetics*.)

Arguing that there are three ways to represent reality – as it is, as it appears and as it ought to be – Aristotle re-interprets mimesis to mean constructing reality as it ought to be, to fashion a reality, in Bacon's words, after the desires of the mind. With reference to the three central questions – the epistemological status of literature, its role in society, and the nature of literary creation – he rejects hyper-literalism and says that poetry need not portray things as they are. There is always an admixture of the "better", of the "ought", of the "possible" and that is how it anticipates human growth and development in excellence. It is imitation yes, but not a distortion – it is a representation of the universal in particular, a superior likeness or image of nature. The "better" in Aristotle's metaphysics is a drive toward the ideal in nature. Universe is no doubt a "flux"; but it is so because it is evolving. Aristotle also reverses Plato's position on the relationship between literature and truth:

> [the historian] describes the thing that has been, and the (poet) a kind of thing that might be. Hence poetry is something more philosophic and of graver import than history, since its statements are of the nature rather of universals, whereas those of history are singulars.
>
> – *Poetics* 9

Aristotle speaks of the disciplining effect of poetry as against Plato's assertion of the deleterious moral effect of poetry. The object of imitation is "men in action" and not just static entities. When Plato considers poetry an inferior art as it involves imitation of what is only an appearance, for Aristotle mimesis is the construction of a signifier that signifies the whole truth of an object as it has its being in its becoming. There is a reversal thus with Aristotle and Homer as the repository of what later came to be recognized as "the poetic truth", is prestiged above Socrates'.

Aristotle's defence produced echoes through the Western critical tradition. Horace celebrates the poet as a preceptor of humanity. In the sixteenth century, Sidney exalted the poet above the philosopher and the historian.

Wordsworth says:

> . . . Aristotle, has said, that poetry is the most philosophic of all writing; it is so: its object is truth, not individual and local, but general and operative . . . truth which is its own testimony. – Preface

Shelley says in *A Defence of Poetry*:

> . . . to be a poet is to apprehend the true and the beautiful. . . . Poets are the unacknowledged legislators of mankind.*

* It is a response to Plato's preference of the legislators, Charondas and Solon, over Homer.

In its continuous engagement with this question, the Western tradition has gone with Aristotle and takes its literature very seriously – witness, for example, the large body of literary exegeses, particularly in the modern period. The assumption of language representing a pre-existing reality is based in the understanding that language is writing and that language is representational. This conception of language breeds what may be called the "scriptal illusion" – it is an easy move from the concrete reality of the visible marks on the page to an assumption of the reality of what is denoted by the visible marks.

The Indian thinkers did not fall into this trap; there is an ancient understanding that language is constructivist, i.e. it constructs the reality rather than representing it. The question then is not whether the verbal compositions are statements of knowledge or not – of course they are, for knowledge and reality are constructed in language: "language cuts forms in the ocean of reality", says the *R̥gveda* (I.164.45). The *Māṇḍūkyopaniṣad* says "all this is *śabda* (*akṣara*)". Ādi Śaṅkara defines the object of all knowledge as that which becomes known through *vāk*: (*sakalavāgagocarma*) and that "all this *jagata* that is cognizable through speech and mind is *sattā* (true)" (*Vivekacūḍāmaṇi* 392). In the Upaniṣadic understanding, language (speech), being rooted in the life-breath and the mind is identical with one's self and consciousness and as such it constitutes the reality for us and the reality so cognized and constituted is *sattāsvarūpa* (of the nature of tru.h). This uninterrupted thinking later develops into a fully coherent theory of Bhartr̥hari who explicitly asserts that all meaning and all difference is constructed by language and that all this *jagata* is a *vikalpa* (specific construction), the *pariṇāma* of language (*Vākyapadīya* 1.118-120). In fact, Bhartr̥hari says there is no knowledge that is accessible except through language: *jñānam sarvama śabdena bhāṣate* (*Vākyapadīya* 1.123).

Therefore, in Indian thought the debate has a different focus – there is no doubt that all verbal discourse is a discourse of knowledge. The effort therefore is to characterize the nature of knowledge in the literary discourse and to evaluate the literary discourse *vis-à-vis* other rational discourses.

A number of typologies have been set up to classify discourse types and to place literature in a cline of authenticity. In the Indian context of orality, literature has been an act of public communication, a performance. That is why all literature is classified as either *śravya* (aural) or *prekṣā* (visual) or both. It is the oral tradition that accounts for the massive body of narrative literature in India. The word used for literature is *vāṅgmaya* – that which has a being in language, that is verbal discourse – underlines the orality of the literary compositions. India has the world's earliest poetry (*R̥gveda*) and the earliest prose (Brāhmaṇas) and the largest body of literature ranging from lyrics to philosophy, astronomy, mathematics and myths. This massive body of literature has in turn generated considerable theoretical thinking about verbal discourse. Several typologies were developed both to characterize different discourses and to establish a mutual order among them.

Most of these typologies place literature at the end of a cline of authoritativeness. To begin with, a basic opposition is made between Śāstra, a composition/treatise meant to be used for teaching a discipline, and *kāvya* (a literary composition): Śāstra for *jñāna* and *kāvya* for *ānanda*. But this is too simple a division and fails to account for the epics like *Mahābhārata* that are traditionally considered to be repositories of knowledge. However as a broad division based on the overall purpose – education vs. entertainment – it is a very valid opposition: philosophical systems which come under Śāstra are certainly studied differently. There is then another typology, an opposition between *apauruṣeya* and *pauruṣeya*. This separates the Vedic compositions from all the rest. It is a knowledge typology – *apauruṣeya* discourse is non-contingent, that is its assertions like those of science are not dependent on an individual for their truth. This body of literature serves in fact as *pramāṇa* for statements in other discourses. As against this, the truth of literary assertions is contingent on the individual. Yet another typology places literature third in the order of authoritativeness. Śruti–Smṛti–Kāvya typologies based on the sources of knowledge – knowledge contained in the Śrutis has been apprehended directly; when and by whom are not pertinent. These are autonomous compositions. *Smṛti* literally means memory. Smṛti texts are products of recall – the knowledge contained in them was already available and it has been put down in an organized text by some thinkers. Kāvya texts construct meanings based on the individual's understanding. Pāṇini, the great grammarian, modifies and extends this typology into a refined fivefold system: *dṛṣṭa–prokta–upajñāta–kṛta–vyākhyāna*. The first category corresponds to *apauruṣeya* and Śruti except that it renders its knowledge still more authentic by replacing the epistemological parameter of "heard" (*śruta*) by the stronger epistemology of "seen" (*dṛṣṭa*). *Prokta* discourse re-enounces a body of knowledge constituted earlier by someone else. Upaniṣads belong to this category. *Upajñāta* texts are systematizations of existing knowledge by another known thinker who however is not the source of this knowledge. *Kṛta* literally means "composed" and Pāṇini mentions as examples some imaginative compositions such as *Mahābhārata* and Yayāti. And Pāṇini adds a new class of literature – the commentary literature (*vyākhyāna*). Finally, there is available in the tradition a threefold classification of statements: *prabhu sammita–suhṛda sammita–kānta sammita*. First, we have statements that have the status of laws – such are the statements of science. Their language and meaning both are inviolate. Statements in Śruti literature belong to this class. Second, we have the statements whose actual words are not so important as the (intended) meaning. Such are the statements of a well-wisher in which case it is the *bhāva* (the intended meaning) that matters. The assertions of Itihāsa–Purāṇa have that status.

Third kind of statements is of imaginative compositions – ideas are fancifully conceived and the language is charming and the statements are not to be weighed for their accuracy or profundity – "I shall pluck stars from the sky and decorate your bodice", says the young lover. It is the craft or archedness in the suggestion or in the expression or in the idea itself that is of interest.

Thus we have a series of typologies in which literature appears low as a discourse of knowledge. But Bharata talking of *prekṣā* forms (drama) says this is "the fifth Veda". Vyāsa also in the very first chapter of the *Mahābhārata* calls the epic "the fifth Veda". The point of these statements is that literary compositions are as much statements of knowledge as the Vedas. Bharata talking of literature as a discourse of knowledge says that it ensures

> righteousness . . . and shall provide guidance to ordinary people in the conduct of life and also help them have serious thoughts (*śāstrīyārtha*). – *Nāṭyaśāstra* 1.14-15

Kuntaka says: "Śāstra eradicates *avidyā*; Kāvya eradicates *aviveka* (lack of discrimination)". In this way it enables the fulfilment of four ends of life – self-knowledge, right conduct, worldly meaningfulness, and psychic fulfilment. Literary discourse achieves this by making the serious thoughts of philosophy accessible in a reader-friendly form – *sarasa artha*. The literary theorists believe this and almost everyone of them underlines the need for an author to be a learned man, with full knowledge of the Śāstras. It is so because one of the clearly recognized goals of literature is making the abstruse knowledge of Śāstras, Smṛtis accessible to common people. In fact, Bhāmaha says that knowledge finds its justification only when it is transmuted into poetry and put within the reach of ordinary people. It is on account of this requirement of disseminating knowledge among the common people that for Bhāmaha simplicity and clarity is the supreme value of literary discourse. If knowledge is not thus transferred, it is "like the pauper's charitableness" (*Kāvyālaṁkāra* 1.3). All learning, he says, must subserve the ends of poetry – such is the poet's responsibility (5.4). Rājaśekhara said much later:

> Kāvya and Śāstra have a relationship of mutual instrumentality; Kāvya serves the ends of Śāstra and Śāstra serves Kāvya. The compositions of a poet who is learned in Śāstras are thoughtful, lucid and excellent.
>
> – *Kāvyamīmāṁsā* ch. 5

Talking about the nature of literary meaning, Rājaśekhara says that in one view, literary compositions are not to be taken seriously because they often talk of (i) untrue (*asatya*), (ii) non-coherent/contradictory (*asaṅgata*), and (iii) ornamental/figurative (*alaṁkārika*) things such as "fame rebounding after striking the four directions"/"bird thou never wert", "it was the best of times, it was the worst times", and "making the sky white"/"the effulgence of a thousand suns". Rājaśekhara contests this by saying that these are characteristic modes of literary expression and that these modes are employed in different degrees by other rational discourses as well, for example, the philosophic and the technical, and that it is always possible to establish the coherence and meaning of such statements. He says that the symbolic mode is an ancient method widely employed in all discourses, including the Vedas and Śāstras. The mode of exaggeration is *arthavāda* in the Mīmāṁsā system, a form of praise, which is not to be taken literally but to be interpreted for its intended meaning. Rājaśekhara argues that such exegesis is required for all reflective discourse and cites in support the well-known Upaniṣadic hymn, *dva suparṇa* . . . (two birds sit on the self-same branch of a tree; one eats the fruit, the other watches) a transparent statement with a picturesque meaning on the surface and also one that figuratively evokes the two selves present in each one of us, the experiencer (*bhoktā*) and the observer (*sākṣī*), a meaning that has to be worked out through careful exegesis.

A distinction is made between two kinds of literary meaning – (i) carefully deliberated and expressed, and (ii) fancifully conceived and fancifully expressed. The fanciful mode must not mislead us into treating literary discourse as a trivial exercise. The meaning in literary discourse has its sources after all in the metaphysical and literary texts and the disciplines of learning of that culture. Rājaśekhara notes nine such sources (*Kāvyamīmāṁsā*, ch. 9) – patronymic texts such as the Bible/Vedas; texts of social codes and conduct such as the Dharmaśāstras/Aristotle's *Ethics*; Itihāsa/history; Purāṇas/mythology; texts of philosophy and other sciences; texts of polity and economy; actual life and experience; literary writings; and the sixty-four arts and crafts such as music, dancing, carpentry, magic, pottery, medicine and astrology. So literary compositions derive their ideas from learned sources and the authors are expected to be men learned in what Vāmana designates as

> the auxiliaries of *kāvya* – (a) the world (*loka*), (b) the sciences, and (c) miscellaneous. . . . By world (*loka*) is meant the operation or action of the world (of animate and inanimate beings). By "science" is meant . . . the science of words (grammar), lexicons, prosody, the arts of singing, dancing, painting and the like, the science of erotics and the science of politics. . . . The miscellaneous consists of – (a) Being acquainted with works of others; (b) engaging oneself in the practice of composition; (c) attendance upon a teacher capable of imparting instruction; (d) careful insertion and

deletion of words; (e) developing the power of composition; (f) one-pointedness or deep concentration of the mind.

It is clear that literary composition is a serious thoughtful activity. According to Rājaśekhara the highest kind of poetry is philosophic poetry and there are three ways in which philosophy is integrated with poetry: there are philosopher poets who:

i. create a new Śāstra in verse. For example, the Vedic seers, the Upaniṣad thinkers and Ādi Śaṅkara in his *Bhaja Govindam* and *Vivekacūḍāmaṇi*.

ii. incorporate literary elements into philosophy. For example, Bhartṛhari in his *Vākyapadīya*.

iii. incorporate philosophical ideas into their literary composition. For example, Vālmīki.

One must also remember that themes and subjects of literary compositions encompass even those areas of reality which involve imaginative construction – consider for example the modern space fiction or fictions about the nether world, about the world of evil spirits and horror. In the treatment of such subjects, there is no question of verisimilitude. Again, in literature, as in every other discipline, certain conventions develop – conventional declarations and conventional analogies. For example, the crocodiles are found in rivers alone but the Indian poets describe the oceans to be full of them; the *koyal* sings in summer too, but the poets describe it as singing in the spring season alone. According to some theorists, such as Bhāmaha, these deviations are faults (*doṣa*s), but other theorists, Rājaśekhara, for example, defend these poetic conventions on the ground that through these poetic conventions the poets exploit the community's shared mental associations – thus "purity" is always associated with Gaṅgā, "poison" with Lord Śiva, silk with Kāñcī and now oranges with Nagpur. Rājaśekhara points out that such deviations may mark almost anything – class reference, particular reference, reference to attributes or to actions. Referentiality of the literary discourse is also affected by counterfactual statements, by the non-mention of facts and by a part mention of facts, but then mere verisimilitude is not the desired end of this discourse though theorists like Bhāmaha, who was a Naiyāyika logician, thinks that consistency and credibility are the two necessary values of poetry. After enumerating numerous instances of logical failures, Bhāmaha goes on to add that "*kāvya* refers to worldly things (*lokāśraya*) and Śāstra to truth (*tattva*)" (*Kāvyālaṁkāra*, chapter 5). The poets may purposefully deviate from the way things are. Rājaśekhara puts forward this principle of literary proposition-making:

> Appearance is not the essential property (*dharma*) of an object. Yet appearance of an object is often sufficient to describe that object, both in Śāstra and Kāvya.
>
> – *Kāvyamīmāṁsā*, chapter 9

So, the question is whether statements in literature should be merely meaningful (*sārthaka*) or that they should be charmingly meaningful, i.e. isn't the manner as important as meaning in literature?

To sum up: *Sārasa artha* – that is the nature of literary meaning. That is how literature disseminates among common people the knowledge embodied in the Śāstras, a knowledge which is otherwise accessible only to a few erudite people, as Bhāmaha says only the unintelligent are afraid of the Śāstras – it is the proper function of Kāvya to make the knowledge of Śāstras palatable – *sarasa*. Vyāsa says that in the ancient times when the four Vedas – the repositories of knowledge in the Indian tradition – were weighed against the *Mahābhārata*, the *Mahābhārata* proved weightier. So Bharata calls literature the "fifth Veda"; Viśvanātha says that Kāvya equally with Śāstra helps attain the four ends of life; Bhāmaha wants the author to be a man learned in the Śāstras and considers poetry as a product of higher intelligence; Rājaśekhara talks of the mutual instrumentality of Śāstra and Kāvya. Finally to describe the singers of the Vedic hymns as *ādikavi* is to accord, by implication, a certain status to Kāvya as an authoritative statement of knowledge.

So knowledge in literature merits attention. We talk of two kinds of *jñāna* in literature. Literature is like a lamp – when lighted, it reveals itself and also the objects around it. In the same way, a poem or a literary composition is both an ontology and an epistemology, it is both an object of knowledge and also a means of knowledge. As a means of knowledge, it makes reference to the world outside itself and as an object of knowledge, it constitutes in itself a segment of human experience. There are thus two aspects of a literary composition – its referentiality (the reference it makes to the world outside and its experiential content (the world/ experience it creates within itself). For example, Sylvia Plath's poem "Daddy" through its host of historical, geographic and cultural references is a "revealer" in one of its aspects – we read and refer to sources outside the poem and collect information. At the same time, the deep pathos, the complex experience of a daughter's irreversible separation from her dead father is "revealed" to us inside the poem. These two aspects are being separated by us as a heuristic comprehending device – in actual fact the two are inseparable in that the internal experience is immanently present in the universe of objects and events as constituted in the composition.

As object of knowledge, a literary composition embodies some human experience which is analysable, in the Indian theoretical frameworks, as a *rasa-bhāva* structure. The Upaniṣad says – *raso vai saḥ* (all this is *rasa*) and Bharata says the *rasa* is the meaning of a text. Experience in a literary text is a *rasa-bhāva* structure, a structure of states of being. *Rasa* is "(state of) being" and *bhāva* is "that which brings about a state of being". The argument is that the being of an individual is a configuration of the *saṁskāras* (traces/impressions) left on us by events (necessarily involving persons) in the form of "emotional conditions/responses". *Bhāvas* springing from an interaction of persons and events constitute experience that shapes our being. They filter into us through our *antaḥkaraṇa* (our cognizing self, a structure of *mana, buddhi* and *citta*) and constitute our self. Our existing being's response to the *bhāvas* transforms/reshapes the being itself resulting in a constant tension between being and becoming. The *rasa*-theory is built around the concept of *bhāva*. In abstract, it looks like this:

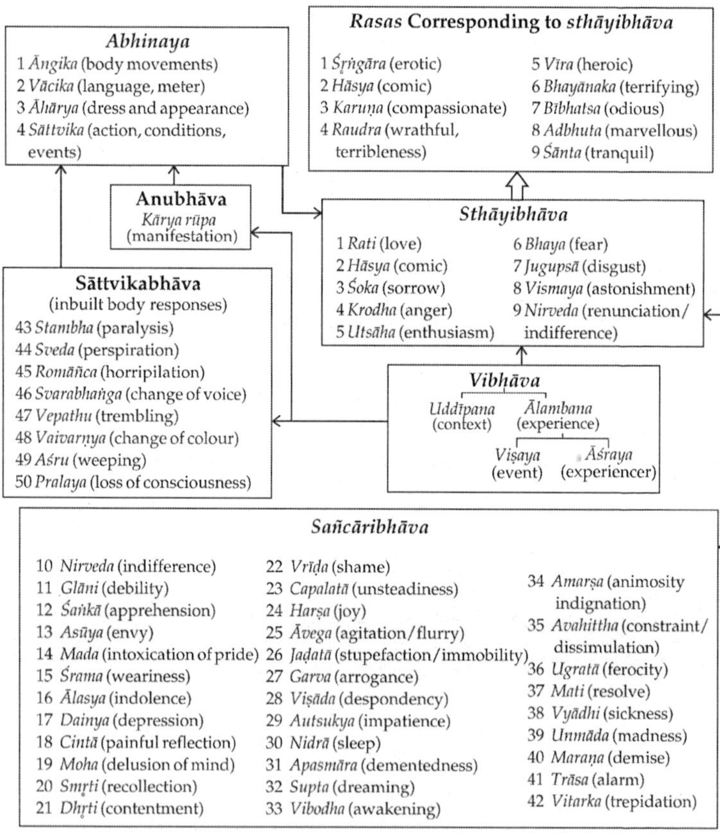

We can understand with reference to Chekhov's popular story "Grief". Iona Potapov (substratum, *āśraya*) experiences grief (*śoka . . . a sthāyī bhāva*) on account of his young son's death (*viṣaya* . . . a generating cause). Both Iona and the son's death constitute *vibhāva* in this theory. Iona's condition – his grief – is accentuated by his memories (Smr̥ti) and by the indifference he suffers among others. These memories and the indifference are *vyabhicārī bhāvas* that serve as auxiliary states (*sañcārī bhāvas*). As a result of his grief, Iona becomes immobile/paralysed (*anubhāva*). The reader experiencing/participating in Iona's grief experiences in turn *karuṇa-rasa* (compassion) and feel deeply another person's grief – something extraordinary and for the moment, the auditor becomes nobler than himself, transcends his small self and feels the suffering of the other as his own. This, says Abhinavagupta, is *mokṣa* (a liberation) from the bounds of one's narrow self and Iona's grief would finally transform him also into a compassionate man.

It is this kind of experience of states of being which constitutes the meaning of a literary text. The meaning of "Michael" is the sorrow of the old father; the meaning of "Waiting for Godot" is the absence of all the positive states of being, the *vibhāvas* of grief producing not grief but disgust.

As an epistemology, literature is a complex category. There are, in fact, two epistemologies in the poem – the poet's and the reader/auditor's. Literary compositions are results of the poet's urge to represent what he has experienced. In the representation, the poet's epistemologies are the ordinary one's – perception, inference, analogy. The whole experience is enclosed in memory.

However, as the representation is in language, or should we say that the constitution of the experience is in language, the reader/auditor's epistemology is only *śabda*. Initially for the auditor there are marks on the page or sounds in the air.

The sounds or the marks refer to the objects which are non-present for the reader/hearer and have to be visualized by him. Abhinavagupta argued that though *kāvya-jñāna* (knowledge in literature) is *śābdika-jñāna* (knowledge through words), it has the same status as *pratyakṣa-jñāna* (knowledge from direct perception). That is when we hear or read a composition, the words virtually make us "see" and "hear", etc. But there is a difference – the image of an object evoked by a word is different and relatively indeterminate, unstable as compared to the image that is created directly on our retina by an object. This mental imaging (*manas vyāpāra*) varies with the different subjects and therefore the "meaning" in literature varies from one hearer to another. We are constantly called upon to fix the reference of the designating expressions. There is much merit in the Indian theorists' category of *parokṣa jñāna* (knowledge of the non-present) – which is what literary knowledge is. The reconstruction of meanings/reference is highly unstable. We as hearers/readers create pictures in our mind – but no two hearers will have the same picture – this is empirically verifiable. The image of a horse differs from the image of a horse evoked by the word "horse". At the end of "Grief", we are informed: "Iona's feelings are too much for him and he tells the little horse the whole story." Is Iona standing or sitting near the horse? What is a little horse? Is he looking at the horse while telling the story? Each reader has a different "understanding".

What is true of objects is more strongly true of ideas and feelings. The *śābdika jñāna* (knowledge constituted in language) must remain a distinct epistemological category different from perception, inference, etc., because what we cognize is a representation, an enactment of and not the object. In *dṛśya kāvya* (drama) it is different – there is a representation there too and *A* stands for *B* but

> . . . the drama is not a creation of the word alone . . . of course the language spoken on the stage is an essential element . . . but the drama is, in addition and more importantly, a visual spectacle; . . . the dramatist represents . . . human actions and events directly by means of characters, gestures, actions, the realm of immediacy is made available through the actor, a crutch upon which the verbal poet is unable to depend.
>
> – E. Gerow 1971: 75

In *śravya kāvya*, on the other hand, words stand in for objects. The words carry all the load. This linguistic representation creates a certain indeterminacy, a complex referentiality, a general tone of suggestion. The Indian theorists claim that the figurative mode, the indirectness of meaning are the defining properties of literary compositions. That *viśeṣaṇa* separates literature from other rational discourses. That the language of literature is "by nature and design not literal" is "the most canonical difference" (Gerow 1971): The modes of cognition are borrowed from/shared with logic and grammar – *sādṛṣyatā* (similarity) or *virodha* (contradiction), for example, but the literary use of these is different. As has been said, "the poetry consists in the misuse of the form". As Bhāmaha has said ". . . the lie is called simile". The poetic expression may be false but it does not serve the ends of falsehood. Logical structures are not absolutely disregarded. Thus discussing *virodha* (contradiction), Ruyyaka says a *samādhāna* (a resolution of the contradiction) must take place – if there is no resolution, it is a flaw (*doṣa*).

So far we have talked of problems of literary representation as a means of knowledge. We have assumed that it is the literary use of language that generates these problems of reference and interpretation, that otherwise language is a perfect fit for objects, and that a one to one correspondence obtains between words and objects. The assumption is too strong. Language, in fact, as Bhartṛhari takes care to point out, is asymmetrical with reality – language is discrete and sequential (*sa-krama*) while reality, is *a-krama*. While thought is a non-sequential whole, its expression is not. Further from one point of view, language creates difference (*bheda*) where none exists, from another point of view, language conceals differences. In its common nouns, language is a generalizing process that puts together a number of separate entities into single classes. On the other hand, lexical distinctions impose themselves on entities that are ontologically not distinguishable – "bush" and "tree", for example. Through the process of naming, discreteness and sequentiality, the two properties of language get imposed on and appear as necessary attributes of the reality when language is used to talk about this reality. The dominant theory of meaning again claims that meaning again is subjectively constituted, that it is a mental construct (*bodhārtha*). Words refer to universals or particulars; they affirm something positive or exclude what the object is not; they refer directly to objects or through mental mediation? What is the role of a speaker's *vivakṣā* (intention) in the constitution of meaning? All these dimensions of linguistic meaning contribute towards making linguistic statements either ambiguous or opaque or contradictory or tautological or polyvalent or apparently meaningless. Such textual indices or situations abound in literary discourse and make it richly meaningful and at the same time indeterminate.

In this sense, the validity of literature as a discourse of knowledge is constrained by its medium, language. The knowledge constituted is linguistic (*śābdika*) an indirect knowledge of the non-present. It does not fall into any of the familiar categories of knowledge – it is not categorical knowledge (*samyak jñāna*); it is not doubtful knowledge (*saṁśayātmaka jñāna*); it is not false knowledge (*mithyā jñāna*). Says the great theorist Abhinavagupta, drawing his inspiration no doubt from the grammarians' tradition, particularly Bhartṛhari, that words are mere indicators or signs (*saṅketas*) and as such the knowledge they constitute is *vilakṣaṇa jñāna* (knowledge constituted by specific characterization) a kind of symbolic knowledge. In the same manner, the delight (*ānanda*) is also special – it is neither the worldly joy (*viṣayānanda*) that we get from the fulfilment of our physical desires, nor is it the spiritual joy (*brahmānanda*) that follows liberation of the self. It falls somewhere in between and combines in itself something of both the material and the spiritual joy.

Creativity and Creative Process

This issue is pertinent for all artistic activity. Is the artist a "creator" on the analogy of God? Or, is an artist a craftsman? If he is a "maker" or a "creator", then he is a divinely inspired being, and the work of art is an outcome of inspiration and the actual creation is a spontaneous, unpremeditated act.

If the artist is a craftsman, he is free and active in relation to his work; if a creator, he is only an instrument (of divine inspiration) – "make me thy lyre", Shelley says.

So the creative processes involved in the two conceptions are different – in the "creator" conception, making of a work of art is a supra-rational activity; in the craftsman concept, it is a rational activity – art is an exercise of reason. In the other case, it is an expression of a psychic vision.

The issue is – what is the "natural capacity" in a *kavi*? In other words, what are the sources of creativity? Learning or knowledge (*vyutpatti*) is one factor. It is asserted that wide and varied knowledge (*bahujñāta* and *vividha jñāna*) is necessary for a *kavi* because in his compositions "he has to describe any number of subjects" (Rājaśekhara's *Kāvyamīmāṁsā*, chapter 5). Two other factors have been suggested – *pratibhā* (innate ability) and *abhyāsa* (practice) and the fourth factor that has been mentioned in the tradition is *samādhi* (heightened consciousness) obtained through deep mental concentration.

Theorists differ about which factor is primary or indispensable – *pratibhā* or *vyutpatti* – and about the role these factors have in the process of composition. Three positions are taken:

1. *Pratibhā* alone is the source of composition.
2. *Vyutpatti* and *abhyāsa* alone can be the source of poetry.
3. *Pratibhā, vyutpatti* and *abhyāsa,* all the three are *kāvya-kāraṇa* (the sources of composition).

Pratibhā is an innate faculty – a predisposition. All activity of living beings is preceded by this *pratibhā* – it is the faculty that changes the male cuckoo's voice in spring and makes it possible for birds to build nests (Bhartṛhari, *Vākyapadīya* 2.149). This faculty may be a *saṁskāra* from previous births (i.e. a genetic endowment) or is produced here and now by the example and guidance of others or by a study of Śāstras and *kāvyas* (Rājaśekhara, *Kāvyamīmāṁsā,* chapter 4). Functionally, this ability is of two kinds – (1) *kārayitrī,* the ability to put/ represent one's felt experience in words and other devices of communication, and (2) *bhāvayitrī,* the ability to feel and understand the experience to be put in the composition.

Vāmana and Pt. Jagannātha believe that *pratibhā* alone is the source of compositions. Vāmana says that in *pratibhā* lies the very seed of poetry (*Kāvyālaṁkārasūtra* 1.3.16). Pt. Jagannātha says only *pratibhā* (and not *śakti, nipuṇatā* and *abhyāsa* all three as believed by earlier scholars such as Mammaṭa) is the cause of poetry (*Rasagaṅgādhara,* chapter 1), and consists in the prompt recall/appearance of appropriate words and meanings for building up a composition. Also *pratibhā* is a kind of *buddhi* (intellection) that keeps getting new insights and ideas (*Rasagaṅgādhara,* chapter 1). Once you believe that *pratibhā* alone is the source of poetry, you are arguing that poets/writers/composers are born – not trained.

On the other hand, Daṇḍin seems to allow that some kind of poetry may be the product of *vyutpatti* and *abhyāsa*, though for excellent poetry, *pratibhā* is indispensable:

> An inborn genius, learning quite free from defects, and no slight application, these constitute one cause of this excellence in poetry.
>
> Even though there be not that extraordinary gains which depend upon the [specific] nature of the earlier latent impressions, yet speech, cultivated with study and effort, certainly grants her own rare favour.
>
> – *Kāvyādarśa* 1.103, 104

But the most widely agreed position is that all the three factors – *pratibhā, vyutpatti* and *abhyāsa* – together constitute the source of poetry:

> Poetic genius, knowledge born of a study of the world, of sciences and of poems, and the practice of the teachings of those versed in writing poetry – these three together constitute the source of poetry. – Mammaṭa, *Kāvyaprakāśa* 1.3

Rudraṭa (*Kāvyālaṁkāra*) uses the term *śakti* (power) for the faculty responsible for literary creation. His definition of *śakti* is that through which several kinds of meanings and appropriate, lucid sequences of words become perceptible. Now this seems to have influenced Pt. Jagannātha's statement of the function of *pratibhā*.

Rājaśekhara, on the other hand, has a very complex theory of sources of creativity. He posits *śakti* as yet another entity, apart from *pratibhā, vyutpatti, samādhi* and *abhyāsa*. His conception is something like this: in literary creation, *samādhi* is the supreme instrument. *Samādhi* is intense concentration/focusing of the mind (*ekāgratā*). When the *citta* (faculty of cognition) is in *samādhi*, it sees meanings. This, says

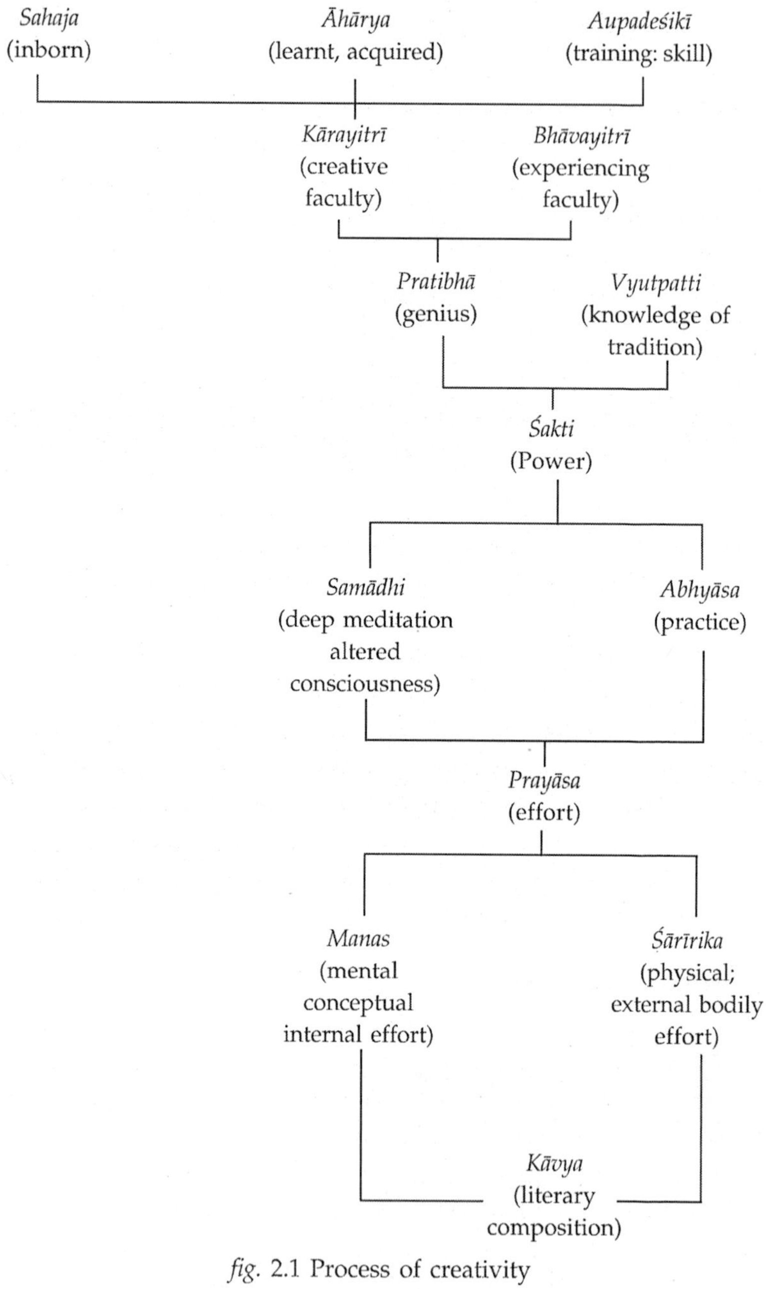

fig. 2.1 Process of creativity

Rājaśekhara, is the view of Śyāmadeva whose work is no longer available. On the other hand, Maṅgala, another theorist, asserts that *abhyāsa* (practice) is the chief source of literary creation.

Rājaśekhara harmonizes these views – *samādhi* is internal/mental effort, while *abhyāsa* is external/physical effort. Together, they generate *śakti* (the power of literary creation). This *śakti* in turn triggers *pratibhā* and *vyutpatti*. *Pratibhā*, as we have already recorded, is of two kinds – (1) *kārayitrī*, the faculty of the poet to create, and (2) *bhāvayitrī*, the ability to appreciate and understand life's experience. *Kārayitrī pratibhā* is then of three kinds – (a) *sahaja* (genetic), (b) *āhārya* (produced by knowledge of Śāstras and Kāvyas), and (c) *aupadeśīkī* (acquired by training). *Fig.* 2.1 reflects Rājaśekhara's theory. This analysis enables Rājaśekhara to classify poets according to excellence.

The relationship to the medium, that is language, is also different. As a craftsman, the poet/writer is the master and manipulates his medium – he creates meaning. As a creator, language is an expression of a reality autonomous of the poet/writer.

In India this issue has been discussed in great detail in the context of iconography. In a community whose dominant philosophy looked upon things perceptible to senses as just *ābhāsa mātra* (mere appearance) it is understandable that no science takes cognizance exclusively of the beauty of perceptible forms and that art never set before itself the object of creating beauty merely of the visible form. What is sought to be represented is *bhāva* – the *tattva* (essence) of being. Thus the Buddha figures do not seek to represent the physical details – instead what they represent is the inner state of mind, Buddha's compassion and deep-seated peace – *karuṇa* and *śānta bhāva*. The anonymous artists, as Coomaraswamy (1957) points out, do not aim to create "beauty", and any "beauty" that appears in the art-object is the beauty that the artist experiences and "reveals" in the object to which his mind attaches itself in adoration, i.e. reverence and love. The dominant Indian world-view (Advaita) predicates the immanence of the absolute, the universal presence of reality. Coomaraswamy talking of the artist's perception of this reality and the consequent revelation of beauty says that this doctrine of the universal presence of reality as the immanence of the absolute (*Brahman*)

> implies that through . . . the world of everyday experience may be seen by those of penetrating vision (artists, lovers and philosophers) glimpses of the real substrate . . . precisely as love is reality experienced by the lover, and truth is reality as experienced by the philosopher, so beauty is [this] reality as experienced by the artist . . . in so far as we see and feel beauty, we see and are one with Him [*Brahman*]. . . . This beauty can be experienced in an object of devotion . . . the Absolute is manifested equally in the little and the great . . . we can . . . achieve Beauty . . . only in learning to see those things as they really are, infinite or beautiful. The artist reveals this beauty wherever the mind attaches itself.
>
> – 1957: 42, 43, 53

Wherever the mind attaches itself, that is the condition of art – and the mind attaches itself, not directly to the absolute, but to objects (Coomaraswamy 1957: 43) which are seen as His reflexes. So the two worlds, of spirit and matter, *puruṣa* and *prakṛti*, are one (Coomaraswamy 1957: 43). It is one undivided all, as illustrated by what Heimann calls

> the well-known metaphor of the spirit riding as a mere passenger in the chariot of the cosmic urge . . . the body is the vehicle, the objects are the course, the material sense organs are the horses, while the intellect . . . is the driver, the Spirit being merely a spectator. – 1937: 41

This explains the coexisting faith in the dogma of plurality and the principle of one universal spirit (monism).

As the object, like all objects, is imbued with *brahman*, the artist's mind attaches itself to the object in reverence and love. This is the Indian understanding of the creative process, the conception of art as *yoga*. *Yoga* is the system of altering/heightening/unifying consciousness by ridding the *citta* (mind) of all *vṛtti*s (cognitions, impressions) through intense mental concentration that merges the subject–object and eliminates the instrument, i.e. the sense, from the process of *jñāna* (knowledge). Art is the product of such a *yoga*, of the yoking of the artist's mind to the object.

Coomaraswamy (1957) explains this concept by reporting the process of image/idol-making as it has been described in the Indian texts. After making the initial observation that "a purely abstract philosophy or psychology like that of early Buddhism does not demand aesthetic expression", he adds:

> It was the spirit of worship which built upon the foundations of Buddhist and Vedāntic thought the mansion of Indian religion, which shelters those whom purely intellectual formulae could not satisfy.
>
> – Coomaraswamy 1957: 29

He further says:

> In devotional faiths was completed the cycle of Indian spiritual evolution from pure philosophy to pure mysticism, from knowledge to love. – Coomaraswamy 1957: 33

Hence the beautiful temple images, the idols that are visual representations of the artist's conception of the *saguṇa* gods and goddesses. The image that the imager transcribes is a particular image of the god:

> The lineaments of images are determined by the relation which subsists between the adorer and the adored.
>
> – Śukrācārya quoted by Coomaraswamy 1957: 176-77

What is the creative process involved in this conceptualization and then its transcription or representation? The artist's concentration on the object of his creativity is an analogue of the yogic meditation (*samprajñāta/savikalpa samādhi*):

> Let the imager establish images by meditation on the deities who are the objects of his devotion. . . . In no other way, not even by direct and immediate vision of an actual object, is it possible to be so absorbed in contemplation, as thus in the making of images.
>
> – Śukrācārya quoted by Coomaraswamy 1957: 26

This practice of visualization, it is pointed out, "is identical in worship and in art" (Coomaraswamy 1957: 27). Coomaraswamy (1957) then takes an example from Buddhist sources to explicate the artist's meditation. There are seven well-marked stages:

1. The artist (*sādhaka, yogin*) ceremonially purifies himself (cf. Patañjali's *Yogasūtra* 2.1-28).
2. He withdraws to a solitary place.
3. There he offers daily acts of worship to the deities and the deity.
4. He "must realize in thought the four infinite moods of friendliness, compassion, sympathy and impartiality".
5. Then he must meditate on the vast emptiness (*śūnyatā*). (This idea of the abyss destroys the *ahaṁkāra*, the ego-consciousness.)
6. Then "he should invoke the desired divinity of the desired utterance of the appropriate *bīja*". (The mystical letter forming the essential part of the *mantra* of a deity.)
7. Finally, on pronouncing the *dhyāna mantra* (description of the personal attributes of the deity), the divinity appears visibly, "like a reflection" or "as a dream".

This image then the artist transcripts or transfers in stone or in words. In words the same creative process holds for the *kavi* – Vālmīki in the Bālakāṇḍa describes an identical process of visualization before setting forth the story of Rāma. Coomaraswamy cites Vasubandhu who in the invocation to Vāsavadatta speaks of the poet "as seeing the world, like a jujube fruit, lying within the hollow of his hands" (1957: 176). The artist in this conception of art and creative process is a pious artisan (Coomaraswamy 1957: 30), a worshipper or a practitioner of meditation (*sādhaka*). He is not a creator – he is a revealer of the inherent *tattva/bhāva*. Now we can make sense of why the Indian tradition of philosophy and literary thinking treats *kumbhakāra* (the potter) as the paradigm artist. The *kumbhakāra* merely fashions forms out of pre-existing substance – he gives *rūpa* to *dravya,* and he does this by shaping (not by measuring, segmenting and cutting as would a carpenter). With his hands he is in communion with the *miṭṭī* (clay) (*dravya*) and in that state of *samādhi,* the "form" in the mind flows through the hands to the clay and the form (*rūpa*) comes alive. The forms (*ākṛti/rūpa*) are inherent in the substance (*dravya*) – the artist reveals (makes manifest or visible) them, i.e. makes it possible for the senses to recognize them.

The relationship between the artist and the object is not one of dominance by the artist – he is not a "creator" in the Indian tradition. He is a *sādhaka* (a worshipper), a *yogī* (an ascetic), a *bhakta,* who is full of love and reverence for the object of his thoughts, and his art is a form of meditation or prayer. The aesthetic experience is a sacred experience. The artist is mentally and spiritually a worshipper and in the actual handling of his material, a craftsman, – the sculptor and the mason alike. So Pāṇini (in *Aṣṭādhyāyī*), while mentioning various guilds of craftsmen, also mentions the poets' guides. One can contrast this conception with the Western conception of the artist as a creator on the analogy of God as the prime creator. In Platonic thought and tradition, the source of the artist's creativity is in divine inspiration. In the Indian thought there are three sources of creativity (vide Rājaśekhara's, *Kāvyamīmāṁsā*) – *abhyāsa* (practice), *vyutpatti* (derivation; study or knowledge of existing art or literature) and *pratibhā* (inborn ability; intuition). The artist has an innate ability, but he must study and become familiar with the practice of the earlier masters, and then he must practise his own art constantly. Indian philosophers, musicians, dancers, architects and poets, all display these three attributes.

3

Categories of Literary Artefacts

Forms/Genres of Literature (Kāvya–Nāṭya Bheda)

Two issues of critical importance in Western literary thinking are:

1. the kind of form – organic or inorganic, and
2. the relationship of literary form to order and to form in life.

Inorganic form is mechanical and external to the content. It is an author's device, an organization imposed by him on his composition. Numerological form, for example, to devote equal number of chapters, say, to different aspects of a theme and to have in each chapter the same number of paragraphs or in a poem, to have a number of sections and in each section the same number of stanzas and in each stanza, the same number of lines is crafting and imposing an order on the materials. As against the mechanical form, there is the biological form – a literary object is envisaged as a living being with a life of its own and as such it has an integral unity of given elements. The structure – birth, growth, decline and death – for example, is a biological structure, and a narrative could be organized to show this pattern. The concept of a literary work as a biological unity originates with Aristotle in his discussion of the parts of a tragedy.

There is yet another possibility – the symbolic form – when, for example, the content is organized and ordered in a metaphor. A good example is Dickens' *Hard Times* where the narrative is organized into an agricultural metaphor – into three spans of "Sowing, Winnowing, Reaping". Highly complex symbolic forms are possible and, from the point of view of language–reality relation, language itself is a "symbolic form", a symbolic representation or expression of life.

The other issue – of the relation between literary form and life – has been important for poets and writers in the twentieth century. The disturbing meaninglessness of life, an absence of any order or system in life, became a dominant awareness in the West during and after the *Armageddon* of First World War. Is an ordered, neatly organized literary narrative a true reflection or image of this essentially chaotic human order? The writers wondered! The answer was "no" for men like Pound and Joyce. James Joyce, in particular, in *Finnegon's wake,* sought to break through the consistency and system of language by disintegrating its syntax so that it could become an adequate expression of the fragmented consciousness and dislocated life.

This conscious creation of chaos, it is asserted by others, is also a kind of order – "formlessness" is also a "form". The term "chaosmos" denotes "the chaotic cosmos" which, come to think of it, however, is a very sensible entity.

Search for pattern or meaning is the basic drive (function) of the human mind. There are visible patterns which are open to perception and there are subtle structures that have to be inferred and reconstructed. Structures of art in this sense are expressions of a basic human drive – they are however "reconstructions" and much more amorphous and subtle than structures, say, in mechanics (physics, for example).

As for genres, Aristotle down, there are basic genres such

as epic, drama, lyric, story and novel. Each has sub-types but no need was felt for any rigorous typology.

In Indian thought, however, there is a much greater proliferation of forms and thus their rigorous sytematization. Several typologies of genres or forms of composition are available in the tradition. The dichotomy such as Śāstra-Kāvya is in fact a forms-divide based on the nature of content, the reasoned, argued knowledge versus creative, imaginative representation of life and experience, and the sub-categories thereof are refined divisions of different domains of knowledge in one case, the Śāstras, and different domains of creative expression on the other. The two share the societal role of imparting values but differ in the way they do it – in a direct discourse and in a discourse in which meanings are indirect.

As noted above, *kāvya* includes metrical and non-metrical, prose and verse compositions. All forms – *nāṭya* (drama), *kathā* and *ākhyāyika* (narratives), and *mahākavya* (epics) – are included under *kāvya*. Bhāmaha says:

> Word and meaning taken together constitute *kāvya*. It is of two kinds, prose and verse. It is further distinguishable into Saṁskrit, Prākr̥t and dialects. – *Kāvyālaṁkāra* 1.16

This is a classification based on language. Next, Bhāmaha gives a classification based on subject matter:

> *Kāvya* is divided, fourfold thus – real narratives of gods, etc., stories put together [fiction], discourse relating to arts (*kālā*) and that relating to Śāstras (treatises of sciences).
> – *Kāvyālaṁkāra*, chapter 1

Then Bhāmaha (*Kāvyālaṁkāra* 1.18, 24-30) presents a classification based on the nature of composition (*fig.* 3.1). This is just a list. The parameters of organization, reader, audience

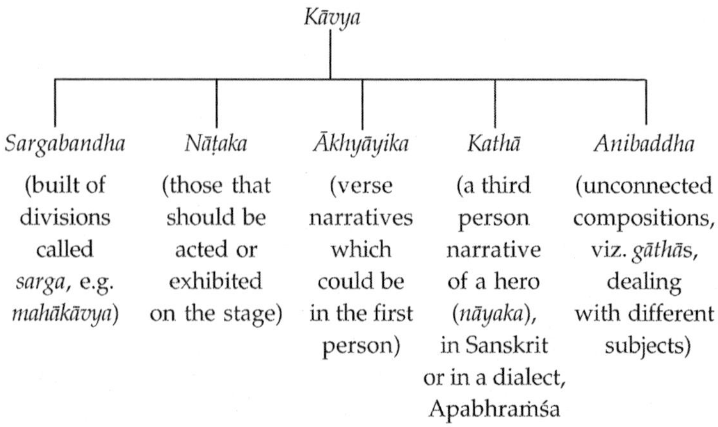

fig. 3.2: Nature of composition by Bhāmaha

interest and narrative structure are treated as equal in this. Daṇḍin later argued:

> *Kathā* and *ākhyāyika* constitute just one species denoted by two names. Herein also are comprised the remaining species of narration. – *Kāvyādarśa* 1.28

What are all the species of narration? On the basis of different theorists, and particularly Bhoja (vide *Śṛṅgāraprakāśa*), the types

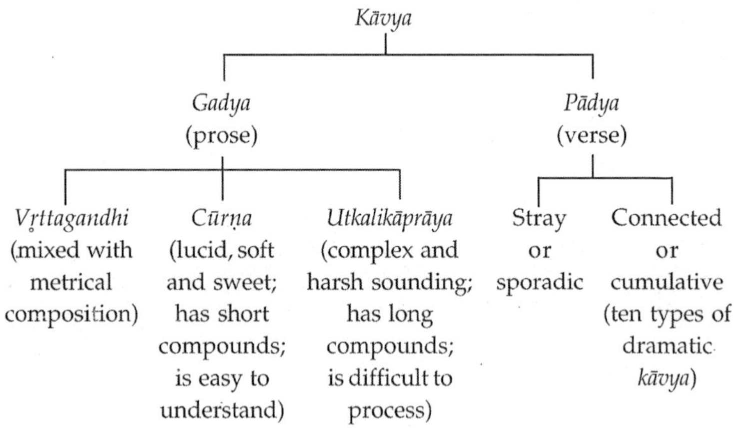

fig. 3.3: Types of narration

identified are given in *fig*. 3.3. Interestingly, Vāmana says that other compositions, narratives, etc. proceed from the dramatic *kāvya* (*Kāvyālaṁkārasūtra* 1.3.32).

What are these ten kinds of dramatic *kāvya* and what are the definitions or major types of *kāvya*? For information on these questions, we go to Viśvanātha, who has done a very comprehensive and systematic classification of *kāvya* and has provided careful definition of each type in *Sāhitya-Darpaṇa*, chapter 6. We present in *fig*. 3.4 the bare outline of his typology.

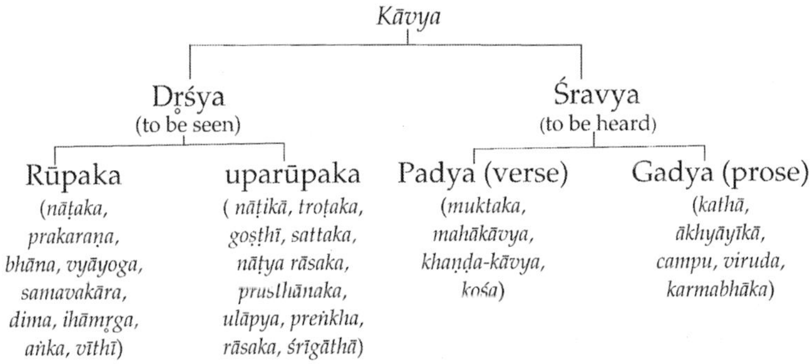

fig. 3.4: Two divisions of compositions

Author/Kavi/Types of Poets

Because Indian culture has been, and is, an oral culture, the conceptual categories of literary theory are rooted in oral composition's renditions and performances and, therefore, many key concepts and issues of Western literary theory are not pertinent to Indian literary experience. Examples that prominently come to mind are the twin concepts of "writer" and "reader", the name "literature" itself, and the issue, for example, of "authorial meaning". The notion of "writing" implicit in the word "writer" renders inappropriate this conception of an author in a tradition of oral compositions. One would rather talk neutrally of a "composer", just as the Greeks talked of a "maker" (*vate*). The word "composer", apart from denoting only a mental process of putting together ideas/ words, has the advantage of suggesting a certain relationship with musical composition, is besides other things, a structure of sounds (speech–sounds), and is therefore assumed to have, in Indian literary theory "an appeal for the ear" aural-interest (*śravya*) which is one of the two major attributes of any literary composition, *prekṣā* (visual interest), being the other. In the same way "reader" is a term that does not apply to the body of Indians for whom literary compositions are intended. We cannot talk of "reading" as the dominant modes of processing a literary text are "hearing" and "watching". So we have a complex processor of literary texts – hearer–viewer. No one term would suffice to describe this complex function. We may appropriate the term "auditor" that Johnson used in his *Preface to Shakespeare* and Shelley uses (*A Defence of Poetry*) to express this complex of functions.

In Western thinking, a literary work has an originator, a man whose creation it is – the poet, the artist. This was the classical view. And the poet/artist was a specially/divinely endowed individual and therefore his creation was authentic. The meaning/message of a work was the author's meaning, the author is the organizer and the source of a literary work, just as God is the source of this universe.

So the author's biography and his manuscripts are very important and indispensable to a proper understanding of the work. The work bears characteristic marks or "signature" of the writer – of his philosophy, his attitude, his characteristic turns of expression. These tell-tale marks unite all the work of a writer into a creative unity.

With loss of faith in God, in the theories of an originator or as the first cause and with post-de Saussure understanding of language as a play of arbitrary signifiers and signified, the author is considered "dead" by some major contemporary theories. What does this mean? Earlier, there was one interpretation of a work tied to the author's intention. Now meaning of a work is "decentred" – any number of interpretations that are plausible can be offered and they don't have to be authenticated by the author's meaning. Author's biography is not important, nor the biography of the text. The manuscripts, with their revisions now, are evidence not of the author's intention but of the play of signifiers. The text is autonomous. A number of new questions are now asked. Does the author always communicate truthfully what he has experienced? Does only the intended meaning get communicated? Do writers consciously mislead the readers? Is language centred in the individual? Is the meaning in language individual or social?

In Indian thought, *kavi* is a learned man who describes some subject/object. In the next phase, the word *kavi* is being given a closer definition: it is no longer sufficient to produce a description. The description must have some special attribute or quality (*camatkāra*) that evokes in the audience some pleasure or delight and has a marked effect. The literary description or language must have some "markedness". With this constraint now, the composers of social metrical texts – such as Manu – are not called *kavi* any more.

Certain abilities are attributed to a *kavi* – he has a special inwardness with words and is able to give extraordinary descriptions of objects, people and themes – *lokottara varṇana nipuṇatā* is how *Rasagaṅgādhara* (chapter 1) describes him. He is also learned in grammar and logic (Bhāmaha, *Kāvyālaṁkāra* 5.4) and has a discriminating intellect. To this Abhinavagupta added the quality of special perception or insight (*Abhinavabhāratī*, the comment on *Rasasūtra*). A *kavi* shapes a new form (*racanā*) by virtue of these abilities – so Brahmā, the creator, is also described as a *kavi*, because Brahmā also reshaped the primordial matter into a form recognizable as this universe. Ānandavardhana adds the dimension of individual will – he says the poet creates a "world" as it pleases him and in his hands the animate becomes inanimate and the inanimate becomes animate, a ruin is transformed into a palace and a palace is transformed into a ruin.

Almost every theorist underlines the *kavi*'s need for learning, his knowledge of Śāstras. It is understandable, for one of the clearly recognized goals of literature is making abstruse knowledge accessible to common people. Bhāmaha says that the knowledge of Śāstra is justified only in a *kavi* – otherwise such knowledge is "like the pauper's charitableness" (*Kāvyālaṁkāra* 1.3). All learning must subserve poetry – such is the *kavi*'s responsibility (*Kāvyālaṁkāra* 5.4). Rājaśekhara says much later:

> Kāvya and Śāstra have a relationship of mutual instrumentality – Kāvya serves the ends of Śāstra and Śāstra serves Kāvya. The compositions of a *kavi* who is learned in Śāstra are thoughtful, lucid and excellent.
>
> – *Kāvyamīmāṁsā*, chapter 5

So, says Bhāmaha:

> The desire to compose *kāvya* should be entertained [only] after learning grammar and the meanings of words and after having served the masters therein and after having studied other works (*kāvya*s). – *Kāvyālaṁkāra* 1.10

But knowledge of Śāstra alone is not enough. Poetry is an intelligent activity no doubt, but it is more than that.

> Poetry, however, [belongs] to him [*kavi*] who has a natural capacity and that too not invariably. – *Kāvyālaṁkāra* 1.5

What is this "natural capacity" in a *kavi* is one factor. It is asserted that wide and varied knowledge (*bahujñāna* and *vividha jñāna*) is necessary for a *kavi*. Two other factors have been suggested – *pratibhā* (innate ability) and *abhyāsa* (practice). And the fourth factor that has been mentioned in the tradition is *samādhi*, heightened consciousness obtained through deep mental concentration.

Take the related question of "authorial intention", which is a major issue in the Western debate about literary meaning. At one time it was believed that the meaning of a text was the meaning intended by the writer – so the exegetical task was to reconstruct the author's intention by taking recourse to biography, i.e. history of the writer, the work and the age. With the death of the author, which followed the death of God in the Christian world in the nineteenth century, this concept acquired new dimensions – it led to an investigation of the very process of composition and it was postulated that the author perhaps exercised no control on his writing and that the texts virtually wrote themselves. Also that the author, an individual, has no existence as an individual, but is in fact a product of conglomerate social factors and circumstances. These are very significant ideas and of value to all. However, the core concept of "authorial intention" does not apply in the Indian literary compositions, which are more often than not characterized by anonymity of authorship. And this is so even when we know that Kālidāsa is the author of *Meghadūta*. But then it is *a* Kālidāsa – we do not know who he was, when exactly was he born, how long did he live, what was his philosophical creed or religious persuasion and what food did he like? The name is no more than a marker and is an equivalent of "X". The Indian world-view does not attach any importance to the individual and the particular, and the Indian mind constantly searches for patterns and paradigms of human experience – hence the marked preference for myth as a narrative mode. This anonymity is a feature of both the Śāstras (philosophical treatises) and Kāvya (imaginative compositions). Since the authorship is anonymous, there is no question of interpreting a literary text in terms of author's intended meaning – instead, the meaning has to be located autonomously in the text itself. No wonder, therefore, that the Indian literary theories are theories that are concerned with explicating how meaning is constituted and through what devices.

On the question of type of authors, we don't come across much in the Western tradition though on the subject of different kinds of critics we have Horace and his admirer Pope. Schopenhauer (1788–1860) in his essay "On Authorship and Style" has some interesting things to say, more like random reflections, about types of authors, statements that show the contemporary concerns:

> There are, first of all, two kinds of authors: those who write for the subject's sake, and those who write for writing's sake. The first kind have had thoughts or experiences which seem to them worth communicating, while the second kind need money and consequently write for money. They think in order to write, and they may be recognized by their spinning out their thoughts to the greatest possible length, and also by the way they work out their thoughts, which are half-true, perverse, forced, and vacillating; then also by their love of evasion, so that they may seem what they are not; and this is why their writing is lacking in definiteness and clearness.

Consequently, it is soon recognized that they write for the sake of filling up the paper,

> and this is the case sometimes with the best authors; for example, in parts of Lessing's *Dramaturgie*, and even in many of Jean Paul's romances. As soon as this is perceived the book should be thrown away, for time is precious. As a matter of fact, the author is cheating the reader as soon as he writes for the sake of filling up paper; because his pretext for writing is that he has something to impart. Writing for money and preservation of copyright are, at bottom, the ruin of literature. It is only the man who writes absolutely for the

> sake of the subject that writes anything worth writing. What an inestimable advantage it would be, if, in every branch of literature, there existed only a few but excellent books! This can never come to pass so long as money is to be made by writing. It seems as if money lay under a curse, for every author deteriorates directly he writes in any way for the sake of money. The best works of great men all come from the time when they had to write either for nothing or for very little pay. This is confirmed by the Spanish proverb: *honra y provecho no caben en un saco* (honour and money are not to be found in the same purse). The deplorable condition of the literature of today, both in Germany and other countries, is due to the fact that books are written for the sake of earning money. Everyone who is in want of money sits down and writes a book, and the public is stupid enough to buy it. The secondary effect of this is the ruin of language.

A great number of bad authors eke out their existence entirely by the foolishness of the public, which only will read what has just been printed. I refer to journalists, who have been appropriately so-called. In other words, it would be "day labourer".

* * * * *

> Again, it may be said that there are three kinds of authors. In the first place, there are those who write without thinking. They write from memory, from reminiscences, or even direct from other people's books. This class is the most numerous. In the second, those who think whilst they are writing. They think in order to write; and they are numerous. In the third place, there are those who have thought before they begin to write. They write solely because they have thought; and they are rare.
>
> Authors of the second class, who postpone their thinking until they begin to write, are like a sportsman who goes out at random – he is not likely to bring home very much. While the writing of an author of the third, the rare class, is like a

> chase where the game has been captured beforehand and cooped up in some enclosure from which it is afterwards set free, so many at a time, into another enclosure, where it is not possible for it to escape, and the sportsman has now nothing to do but to aim and fire – that is to say, put his thoughts on paper. This is the kind of sport which yields something.
>
> Although the number of those authors who really and seriously think before they write is small, only extremely few of them think about the subject itself; the rest think only about the books written on this subject, and what has been said by others upon it, I mean. In order to think, they must have the more direct and powerful incentive of other people's thoughts. These become their next theme, and therefore they always remain under their influence and are never, strictly speaking, original. On the contrary, the former are roused to thought through the subject itself, hence their thinking is directed immediately to it. It is only among them that we find the authors whose names become immortal. Let it be understood that I am speaking here of writers of the higher branches of literature, and not of writers on the method of distilling brandy.

It is only the writer who takes the material on which he writes direct out of his own head that is worth reading.

In the context of the question of poetic creativity, Rājaśekhara classifies poets according to excellence and measurable criteria. And he develops two well-considered typologies of poets. The finest *kavi* (*sārasvata*) has inborn *saṁskāras*, impressions or traces of *pratibhā*, and his works can be heard on the lips of ordinary people round the world (unlike other poets whose compositions are either limited to select audience or even to their own household). Rājaśekhara goes on to describe three kinds of poets:

1. *Śāstra kavi*, one who excels in seriousness of thought.

2. *Kāvya kavi*, one who excels in craft, language and aesthetic effect.
3. *Ubhaya kavi*, one who excels both in Śāstra and Kāvya.

The *Śāstra kavi*s are of three kinds:

(a) One who creates a new Śāstra in verse (the Vedic seers of the Upaniṣads, for example, or Ādi Śaṅkara in *Vivekacūḍāmaṇi*).

(b) One who incorporates literary elements, Kāvya, into a Śāstra (Bhartṛhari in *Vākyapadīya*, for example).

(c) One who incorporates Śāstric ideas in his compositions (Kālidāsa, for example, in his *Raghuvaṁśa*).

The *Kāvya kavi*s, according Rājaśekhara (*Kāvyamīmāṁsā*, chapter 5), may be classified into eight kinds on the basis of poetical qualities.

(a) *Racanā kavi*, one who excels in choice and arrangement of words and whose thoughts do not merit any serious attention.

(b) *Śabda kavi*, one in whose work there is a high frequency of some one part of speech or the other. For example, *nāma kavi* is a poet whose language has a high density of nouns. Similarly, *ākhyāta kavi* is a poet with a high density of verbs.

(c) *Artha kavi*, one who excels in fanciful conceptions/ideas.

(d) *Alaṁkāra kavi*, one who excels in the employment of various figurative devices.

(e) *Ukti kavi*, a poet who excels in telling expressions worthy of being quoted and requoted.

(f) *Rasa kavi*, a poet who excels in evoking different states of mind (*rasa*s).

(g) *Mārga kavi*, a poet who excels in one of the three modes of expression (Gauḍīya or Panali or Vaidarbhī).

(h) *Śāstrārtha kavi*, one who employs technical categories of philosophy in his compositions.

It is argued that these could as well be construed as properties (*guṇas*) of literary compositions – excellences. A poet is to be judged by the number of these qualities present in his compositions. The work of a great poet (*mahākavi*) has all these eleven merits.

From a different point of view, that of attitude to or facility in composition, we have another typology of poets. Rājaśekhara calls them "states" of a poet – a poet may evolve through them or may belong to one of the types. These are easily recognizable in the Indian situation today and are:

- one who goes to an institution (such as Indira Gandhi National Open University New Delhi) to learn the craft of composition;
- one who keeps one's compositions to oneself out of diffidence or fear of faulty composition;
- one who presents one's own composition as that of another out of fear of adverse criticism;
- one who makes one of the ancient poets as one's ideal and composes on the pattern of one's master;
- one who composes short pieces on diverse themes and does not have a central theme to one's work;
- one who composes a *nibandha kāvya*, a major structured work – he is a *mahākavi*;
- one who has the ability to compose different kinds of works, short lyrics/stories and epic/long narratives, with different *rasas* and in different languages – he is *kavirāja*.

These seven are the states of poets who are learned and well-versed in the Śāstras and Kāvyas. Rājaśekhara mentions three other states of those who train themselves in the craft of poetry with the help of aesthetic *mantras* and practices (*Kāvyamīmāṁsā*, chapter 5). Through constant practice, poets mature in their art – one index of maturity of a poet is the confidence with which he uses language and the certainty with which he uses words requiring little or no subsequent amendations:

> Scholars of Śabdaśāstra (science of language) consider maturity of language as that condition in which a word once used does not allow any change.
>
> – Rājaśekhara, *Kāvyamīmāṁsā*, chapter 5

This is interesting, particularly in view of the modern manuscript scholarship which discovers the revisions, often radical, that a poet makes in his composition.

Reader/Auditor

We have noted above that "reader" is a term that does not apply to the body of Indians for whom literary compositions are intended, and we noted that in the context of the orality and performative nature of Indian compositions, the English term "auditor" best captures the roles of hearer, observer and reviewer.

For quite some time, literary theory and criticism were concerned chiefly with the author. In the twentieth century the attention shifted to the readers as part of the larger democratization process. Literary meaning now was the reader's meaning. The text became open as it was no longer tied to *one* originator. It is now accepted that the meaning of a text is the product of a text–reader interaction. So the reader from its earlier passive role, now has an active, creative role in literary communication. He is not just an observer now – he is a participant.

The word "reader" implies a role in a written tradition. And this role is individualistic. One person reads and makes sense of a text. In the oral cultures, there is a collective participation in the text in popular re-tellings and narrations and performances. The role of an auditor in such traditions is more complex, and at the same time more active by virtue of the living transference or enactment of the text. A reader remains the object (even in the revised conceptions).

The creativity implicit in the reading and the auditing processes is now the subject of much research – how and what all, does the reader rebuild, build-in or reconstruct? There are innumerable readers and one work – does this work remain one text in the minds of so many readers, or does it become a multiple, polyvalent, if not a totally fluid text? These are some of the critical questions associated with the concept of a reader.

Consider the relationship that holds between the audience/reader and the object of art. With reference to literature, three distinct stages in the evolution of ideas in this respect can be discerned. In Bharata's *Nāṭyaśāstra*, we have the notion of *prekṣaka* (an observer) an impersonal observer or receiver of the text. In the sixth/seventh century CE, in Bhāmaha we have a revised notion – the notion of *sāmājika* (a social being) and a participant in a collective performance as it were. Finally, in Ānandavardhana, ninth century CE, we get the concept of a *sahṛdaya* (of the same heart); that is, that reader/viewer/hearer who can fully comprehend and appreciate a work of art that has the same intellectual and emotional equipment, the same sensibility, as the artist.

The three stages in the conception of a "reader" are also indicative of the specific relationship that obtains between the text and the audience in the Indian socio-cultural reality. This is a multiple and complex relationship as perhaps one would expect in an oral tradition. The texts are performed, narrated, studied and enounced (ritual enunciation). They are used for education (in *kathā*s, oral recitations/narrations), for ritual purposes (in ceremonies), for crisis management (in situations of distress such as defeat in or prospect of war) and for intellectual advancement (*adhyayana* or study). As against the monistic reader-function in which the modern reader relates to literature in a literate society, in India, a very complex relationship (socio-cultural relationship) obtains between an individual and his texts, and in that complex relationship, the reading function is only a minor function, as most Indians learn their texts through hearing (varied folk, oral performances). For example, more people have become acquainted with episodes from the *Mahābhārata* through Teejan Bai's performances and from the television serial than through individual study. In this perspective of the oral tradition, the visual media, the television and the videos, for example, are perfect instruments of communication and fit in beautifully with the Indian traditions of aural-visual experiencing art and literature. Is it any wonder, therefore, that *Rāmāyaṇa* and *Mahābhārata* were such eminent successes and had more than 90 per cent viewership in India – watching them every Sunday became almost a ritual with the Indian families.

Language of Literature

Three dimensions of the language of literature have come in for discussion:

1. language as a system of representing reality,
2. language as a system of communication, and
3. the characteristic figurativeness of literary language.

Language as a system of representing reality, paradoxically, both creates and conceals difference. When words make a distinction between one bird and another, one plant and another, one object and another, the commonness between them, the fact of their belonging to the same kind of specie is glossed over. At a more conceptual level, the difference lies at the level of visible forms – thus "earrings" and "bracelet" are two forms of the same one substance – gold. Language –

its vocabulary – names visible forms and therefore captures a relatively "superficial" level of reality. On the other hand, the generalizing property of language conceals differences; thus no two apples are alike, but we use the same one word "apple" for all, creating a uniformity which is not real.

Further language is intrinsically asymmetrical with reality – it has discreteness and sequence while life/reality is non-discrete and configurational. So the "structure" of language has the propensity to "structure" the experience it describes or represents.

Language is the most pervasive means of communication. There are three points of view on the nature of language as a communication system: (1) it is a barrier, i.e. it draws a curtain across reality and conceals the truth from us; (2) it is a lens through which we see reality clearly and in sharp focus; and (3) it creates a reality (rather than represent it), i.e. a world is communicated clearly but this world is a heterocosm – an autonomous world of discourse, in which case its relationship to the existing world can be quite indirect – symbolic, for example.

If language is a barrier, then the poet/writer must strive to make it disappear. Literary traditions at one time or the other attach value to obscurity and the writing of those times is often very complex, for example, that of the Great Moderns, Yeats, Eliot, and at other times, sometimes as a reaction, value is attached to, lucidity or simplicity. Simplicity is a major value of classicism in art. Simplicity, however, must be kept apart from simpleness – simplicity, is achieved through a complete mastery of what one wants to say and of language.

Finally, the characteristic property of literary language, is its figurativeness – the meaning is almost always either indirect or more than what is directly expressed. Critical attention has been given to various figural devices – metaphor, irony, image. Figurativeness separates literary discourse from other rational discourses.

Literature is verbal knowledge (*śābdika-jñāna*). Literary compositions are results of the need or urge to represent (*anukaraṇa*) what the poet/composer knows or has experienced. In the representation, the poet's epistemologies are the ordinary ones – perception, inference, similarity. The whole thing is enclosed in Smṛti (memory). However, as the representation is in language, for the reader/hearer, the epistemology is *śabda* (language) which relates only indirectly to the ordinary means of knowledge. Initially, for the hearer/reader, there is an elementary perception of marks on the page or sounds in the air. The marks and the sounds refer to objects, in the widest sense, which are actually absent, and have to be visualized. Abhinavagupta argued that though *kāvya jñāna* is *śābdika* (linguistic), it is a form of *pratyakṣa* (perception). That is, when we hear or read a composition, the words virtually make us "see", "hear", etc. But an intrinsic difference remains – the image of an object that a word evokes is different and relatively unstable as compared to the image that an object creates directly on our retina. The mental imaging (*manas-vyāpāra*) depends on and varies with the individual subjects and therefore the meaning in literature, the objects that are designated by even material nouns, also varies from one hearer/reader to another. We are constantly called upon to fix the reference of designating expressions, for example, with respect to Iona Potapov in "Grief", about the old cab driver, we are told that if a whole snowdrift fell on him, it seems as if he would not find it necessary to shake it off. Now what is that kind of appearance? How do we visualize Iona? And what is the size or weight of the snowdrift such that he could shake it off but won't?

All nouns, verbs, quantitative adjectives and adverbs involve perception of the viewer/reader. Often the invitation to exercise different kinds of perception is quite straightforward as, for example, in *The Solitary Reaper.*

BEHOLD her, single in the field,
Yon solitary Highland Lass!

....

O listen! for the vale profound
Is overflowing with the sound.

There are reports of the poet's own perception, but the poet may report not from his perception, but from his recollection (Smṛti), or inference, or even imagination (a mental construction), the poet recollects:

The music in my heart I bore,
Long after it was heard no more.

The poet infers:

Alone she cuts and binds the grain,
And sings a melancholy strain;

The poet imagines:

No nightingale did ever chaunt
More welcome notes to weary bands
Of travellers in some shady haunt,
Among Arabian sands.

The poet's knowledge is uncertain (*saṁśaya*) as in:

Perhaps, the plaintive numbers flow.

Much more than in the reports of the poet's perception, the readers' reconstruction of meaning/reference (*padārtha*) is highly unstable. We as hearers/readers create pictures in our mind, but no two hearers will have the same picture.

Kāvya is *jñāna* (knowledge). For this *jñāna* (*dharma*), *alaṁkāra* (figurativeness) is *dharmī* (attribute or substance). That is, the figural mode is the mode of cognition in *kāvya*. What are the forms that this mode takes – many (sixty-one, according to

Mammaṭa, *Kāvyaprakāśa*, chapter 10). Most of them are borrowed from logic and grammar, though they are redefined in *kāvya*. For example, *sādṛśya* (similarity) is one of the seven categories admitted in Mīmāṁsā. Comparison (*upamā*) is allowed by Nyāya as one of the four criteria of apprehension (Annamabhaṭṭa, *Tarkasaṁgraha*, section on simile). The poetic use of these is however different. As has been aptly said, poetry consists in the misuse of the form. There is an element of impossibility, a certain *vakratā* in the comparison. But *vakratā* must not go beyond a limit – the absurd ceases to be poetry. Bhāmaha's definition of the simile is:

> The [expression of] similitude, in terms of a qualitative aspect, between the subject [of comparison] and an object [of comparison], incompatible with it in place, time, activity, is called simile. – *Kāvyālaṁkāra* 2.30

Poetic expression which is true nevertheless deviates from the norms and standards of literal expression, which is the most usual (or most obvious) apparatus for defining what is true; poetic expression is false, yet it does not serve the ends of falsehood. Logical structures of consistency, etc. are not absolutely disregarded.

It is not true that language is symmetrical with what it represents or is a good fit. This is so on account of five reasons, namely, the very nature of language as a system,

1. the nature of word–meaning relationship,
2. the nature of lexical denotation and sentential meaning,
3. the role of *vivakṣā* and *tātparya*, the speaker's desire and intention, and
4. the role of contexts and conditions.

Literary Meaning and Sources, and Types of Literary Meaning

There are many critical problems associated with literary

meaning. What is the nature of literary meaning? Is the meaning of a text controlled or generated by the author's intended meaning? Or, is the literary meaning a construct of the reader? Or, is the literary meaning autonomous of the author and the reader and constructed purely by the discourse? And there is the still more fundamental problem – is the literary meaning determinable at all? It would be determinable if it is constructed by the language of the text. Or is this meaning open-ended, constantly deferred or shifted as a result of the very nature of linguistic denotation?

What are the sources of ideas in a given literary work? In which all disciplines and areas of history and culture do the ideas of a literary composition originate? A study of this kind can often demonstrate the wealth and welter of ideas in a work.

What are the narrative modes of communicating meaning? For example, one may just describe something or tell a contemporary story or resort to a popular myth or a legend, or construct an allegory or a symbolic narrative. Choice and preferences from among these have to do with the author's craft – the way he composes his text. Again, at different times in the cultural history of a community, different modes may become the preferred modes – for example, the metaphor with the Elizabethans and the symbol with the Romantics.

In literature, one is not always looking for novelty of ideas – more often, that slightly marked perception, the fancifulness of conception that allures the readers. Criticism may explicate this fancifulness.

The two traditions look at this issue from different points of view – the Indian thinkers consider them from three points of view: in terms of the source from where the meaning is drawn – philosophy, worldly life, earlier compositions – and structuring of the meaning, in what mode it is expressed, figurative or literal and how it appeals to the audience. The Western theory considers this in terms of whose meaning it is

– the author's, the society's, the readers' or of God.

Literary statements are often fanciful and literary discourse is almost always figural. The literary world is a construct of one man's imagination. Then how far is the literary discourse reliable as a means of knowledge? What is the validity of literary statements? The poetic mode is often non-coherent, non-truthful (Bird thou never were!) and figurative (hyperbolic) and then there are the literary conventions also. So can literary discourse be taken seriously?

It is argued that "fancifulness" or "charm" is the value of literary art (as of other arts) that makes the ideas or meanings palatable and easy to assimilate. But on account of this "charm", the ideas are not devalued or belined. A writer after all does not invent his ideas. In fact, he may be borrowing his themes and ideas from the community's philosophy, history and culture to build a very rich, substantial discourse. All these ideas are however, modulated in the literary mould – which makes them pleasurable and easy to comprehend.

The truth of literature in relation to the truths of philosophy and history has been a subject of perennial investigation in the Western tradition. The debate has now been capped by the post-Saussurean understanding that "truth is a linguistic question". Lot of people and many governments have taken literary statements seriously – too seriously, in fact. Plato did when he wanted to banish poets from his republic and the Soviet government did in the twentieth century. Books continue to be banned and writers ostracized.

Against this, we have the view that writers and poets wield no influence at all and can be ignored. After all, how many people form their ideas and opinions from literature, from the written/printed work?

In Indian thought, *kāvya* is a dependable source of knowledge (referential world) because learning, training and care go into compositions. Talking of sources of meaning in compositions, Rājaśekhara says that it is traditionally accepted that *kāvya* has its origin in the following sources:

1. Vedas.
2. Smṛti (Dharmaśāstras).
3. Itihāsa.
4. Purāṇas.
5. *Pramāṇa vidyā* (Mīmāṁsā, etc., six philosophies).
6. *Rājasiddhānta trayī* (the three sciences dealing with society and politics – Arthaśāstra, Nāṭyaśāstra, Kāmaśāstra).
7. *Loka* (worldly, pragmatic knowledge).
8. *Viracanā* (compositions – poems, plays, narratives, epics – of other composers).
9. *Prakīrṇaka* (sixty-four arts/crafts, including specially Ayurveda, medicine, Jyotiṣa, astronomy, Vṛkṣaśāstra, botany, Aśvagajalakṣaṇa (zoology).

Composers take whole themes or plots or take some characters or use sporadic ideas from these sources, or, a composition may illustrate or exemplify the truth of some proposition in these sources, or, a composer may draw his *upamāna* (object of analogy) from these sources. In fact, the analogical use is found in abundance.

There is available in *Kāvyamīmāṁsā* a very interesting classification of types of meaning in *kāvya*. This classification is based on the types of objects or beings that are the subject matter of *kāvya*. *Kāvya* may deal with any or all of them, or it may interpret/describe an object/being belonging to one category in terms of an object/being belonging to another category. The seven types of meaning are:

1. *Divya* (celestial/divine). Meaning concerned with

divine/cosmic beings and objects.

2. *Mānuṣa–Divya* (human–divine/superhuman). Meaning establishing a relationship between the celestial and the worldly beings and objects.
3. *Mānuṣa/Mātarya* (human). Meaning related to ordinary human world. This is routine.
4. *Pātālīya* (of, to the nether world). Meaning concerned with creatures of the nether world.
5. *Mātarya-Pātālīya* (pertaining to this world and the underworld). Meaning establishing a relationship between the beings and objects of this world and the nether world.
6. *Divya–Pātālīya* (celestial–nether world). Meaning establishing a relationship between the divine and the nether world beings and objects.
7. *Divya–Mātarya–Pātālīya* (celestial–earthly–nether world). Meaning establishing a relationship among beings and objects of the three *loka*s – celestial, earth and nether world.

There is no limit to such innovative configurations. The universe of meaning is infinite, says Rājaśekhara. But it is divisible into two parts:

1. *Vicaritasuṣṭha* (reflective).
2. *Avicarita ramaṇīya* (charming, not subject to reflection).

Some propositions/meanings become established after much thought. The more one reflects, the more and more meanings or nuances emerge, and this meaning can stand logical examination. Such meanings belong to the first part – *vicaritasuṣṭha* – and are found in scientific treatises, the Śāstras. The other kind of meaning – *avicarita ramaṇīya* – found in *kāvya* is unusual and attractive, and arrests the attention of the hearer/viewers, but does not stand logical examination. The seven types of meaning mentioned above belong to this class. Such statements contradict our knowledge of reality. For example:

> Śrī Hanumān, to cross the ocean, flew across the sky taking on its blue colour and smearing the sky with his own yellow effulgence. – Rājaśekhara, *Kāvyamīmāṁsā*, chapter 9

Now this statement, Rājaśekhara points out, cannot bear reflection – for the sky is in fact without any *rūpa*, without any colour, nor can it take on any colour. Yet this way of saying that Śrī Hanumān flashed across the sky is attractive and arresting – but not literally credible.

We have already noted (on p. 82) that to explain this kind of poetic meaning, Rājaśekhara puts forward a principle of proposition-making. He says:

> . . . appearance of an object is often sufficient to describe that object, both in Śāstras and *kāvya*.

Thus it makes sense to say "the sun is no bigger than a football". So the question is, should the statements in *kāvya* be only *sārthaka*, have meaning in a strict denotational sense, or *sarasa*, imbued with poetic charm? No meaning is in itself with or without charm – it is the way the poet constitutes it that lends it charm. And in the hands of a poor composer, even a meaning potentially rich in poetic charm may become dry and sterile. The *rasa*, poetic delight or relish or its absence, is in the poet's statement – not in the object. *Rūpa* or *guṇa* (beauty or quality/attribute) are not inherent in objects – it is the poet's mode of statement (*uktiviśeṣa*) that makes the object *saguṇa* (endowed with qualities; hence, with form) or *nirguṇa* (formless).

Yet another pertinent classification is presented next by Rājaśekhara (*Kāvyamīmāṁsā*, chapter 9). It is a classification based on the discoursal devices used to establish the meaning.

There are five categories:

1. *Śuddha* (factual description devoid of any story).
2. *Citra* (description expanded with details that are illustrative of the meaning).
3. *Kathokta* (meaning illustrated with the help of narrative (story)).
4. *Saṁvidhānakabhū* (articulating a meaning with the help of an imagined but possible event).
5. *Ākhyānakavana* (articulating a meaning with the help of a legend).

Literary Conventions and Referentiality

Thus, though *kāvya* derives its meanings (themes, etc.) from the Śāstras, its mode of statement (*avicarita ramaṇīya*) is such that many of its propositions are *arthavāda*s, i.e. they assert things that are contrary to or deviate from our knowledge of the world. However, once the purpose of such *arthavāda*s is identified, their coherence (*saṅgati*) gets established. Another source of deviation from the known is *kavisamaya* – the poetic conventions. For example,

> the crocodiles are found in rivers only, but the poets [in India] generally describe the oceans to be full of them; *koyal*, the Indian cuckoo, sings in summer too but the poets always describe this bird as singing in the spring season.
>
> –*Kāvyamīmāṁsā*, chapter 9

Discourse of all kinds develops particular conventions.

So *kavisamaya* is any proposition that is contrary to the Śāstras or to the *lokavyavahāra* (the way things are in the world) and is sanctioned only by the literary tradition. According to some theorists, such deviation is a fault – Bhāmaha, Udbhaṭa and Daṇḍin are included in these theorists. But other theorists say that such deviations have always been a part of *kāvya* and therefore have some function – "the *kavi*s benefit from them" (*Kāvyamīmāṁsā*, chapter 9). Rājaśekhara suggests that such poetic practices are the result of successive poets imitating some original usage. What is not suggested by Rājaśekhara, but what one can infer from examples of *kavisamaya* is that the poets exploit the mental associations that a community shares – thus purity is always associated with Gaṅgā, poison with Śiva, and in our times, pearls with Hyderabad, silk with Kāñcīpuram or Varanasi and oranges with Nagpur. The poets are able to emphasize their desired meaning and communicate it effectively by evoking such shared associations.

Rājaśekhara presents a typology of *kavisamaya* poetic conventions which would enable us to classify deviant meanings. Such deviations are of three kinds, pertaining to the celestial sphere, the earth and the nether world. Of these three, the poetic conventions related to *bhauma* (this world) are the most numerous. Deviations are also of four kinds on the basis of the meanings of words – class, individual, quality and action. These are the cases in which poetic deviations may occur. What forms does the deviation take in these four cases? In each of these, deviation can belong to one of the three kinds – mentioning as existing what does not exist, not mentioning what does exist, and mentioning facts partially, selectively. We give examples of three kinds of deviant meaning with reference to class (*jātirūpa*) meaning:

1. Mention of lotuses in rivers, *jātirūpa asat nibandhana* (for, no lotuses grow in flowing waters).
2. Not to talk about flowers, and fruit of the sandalwood tree, *jātirūpa sat anibandhana* (but only of its fragrant wood/fragrance).
3. To talk of crocodiles only in connection with Gaṅgā, *jātirūpa niyama nibandhana* (though crocodiles are found in several rivers).

In the same way with respect to the celestial world and the nether world, one may (1) mention non-existent or non-authoritative facts, or (2) not mention the known facts, or (3) mention the facts selectively. This is the nature of referential meaning in *kāvya*.

Verisimilitude and Literary Meaning

We have said that *kavisamaya* – building meaning in accordance with poetic conventions – is a fault, *kāvyadoṣa*, according to some theorists. In fact, a strong line of thinking in the literary tradition upholds verisimilitude, consistency and credibility as necessary values of *kāvya*. Almost at the beginning of the tradition, Bhāmaha (*Kāvyālaṁkāra*, chapter 4) lists faults (*doṣas*) which are not desirable in *kāvya*:

1. *Apārtha*, no meaning – e.g. in an utterance which is not complete in itself. For example, ten pomegranates. (We ask ten pomegranates – what?)
2. *Vyārtha*, contradictory meaning – e.g. it is enough if you impose modesty on those superiors who have conquered their senses by their devotion to preceptors. Those who have conquered their senses are modest.
3. *Ekārtha*, redundancy, repetition (unmotivated) of words or of meaning.
4. *Saṁśaya*, doubt (unmotivated) (where the words used produce ambiguity when the speaker intends to produce a meaning which is certain).
5. *Apakrama*, non-maintenance of correlated sequence, e.g. Śiva and Viṣnu wearing/carrying the disk and the trident.
6. *Śabdahīna*, ungrammatical.
7. *Yatibhraṣṭa*, misplaced caesura.
8. *Bhinnavṛtta*, unmetrical.

9. *Visandhika*, failure of Saṁhitā, coalescence.
10. *Deśa-virodhī*, counter-factual – e.g. to describe something as growing/produced in a country where it does not grow. For example, the lush deodars of Ootacamund.
11. *Kāla-virodhī*, transposition of seasons – e.g. the mango trees in full bloom render fragrant the winter winds.
12. *Kalā-virodhī*, statement contrary to known facts of arts and technical skills.
13. *Loka-virodhī*, opposed to ordinary experience – e.g. the froth flowing from the charging horses filled the roads with knee-deep water.
14. *Nyāya-virodhī*, that which does not conform to *artha* and *Kāmaśāstra*, and also ordinary experience – e.g. the wise, old king Vatsa desirous of conquest did not have any spies.
15. *Āgama-virodhī*, opposed to the injunctions of Dharma-śāstras – e.g. a righteous king shown killing an enemy who has laid down his arms.

This is an early emphasis on accuracy of reference and logical statement, intended, one supposes, to save *kāvya* from degenerating into mere entertainment. These faults are faults either of ignorance or poor reasoning ability.

In chapter 5 of his book, Bhāmaha discusses logical failures, e.g. a proposition such as god exists (because he is eternal) is *hetu-virodhī* because the substratum of the inference, god, is unknown, and therefore any quality inherent in it cannot be known. In the same way, one may not make statements that contradict the tenets of one's own school – *siddhānta-virodhī*. The third logical failure is *sarvāgama-virodhī*, contrary to the conclusion of all sciences, e.g. statements like *pramāṇa*s do not exist or that there are only three *pramāṇa*s (means of knowledge). Saying the obvious or what is already well known also constitutes a logical defect, e.g. sound is apprehended by ears. This is called *prasiddha dharma*. A proposition that has an inbuilt contradiction is *pratyakṣa bādhinī*, e.g. fire is cold.

These defects concern *pratijñā*, roughly "conclusion" of logic. Bhāmaha goes on to list faults pertaining to *hetu*, the middle term of the syllogism.

Bhāmaha notes that his exposition of *pratijñā* "involving many varieties having reference to definitions, employment and defect" is based on the Śāstras which constitute "one set of views" (*Kāvyālaṁkāra* 5.32). In the compositions, these terms, *pratijñā*, etc. may also have different significance, for "*kāvya* refers to worldly things (*lokāśraya*) and Śāstras refer to truth (*tattva*)" (*Kāvyālaṁkāra* 5.33). So the *kāvya* statements may purposefully deviate, for example:

> The sky is of the colour of the sword (steel-blue). This sound comes from a distance, . . . Oh! the stability of the great lights [of the universe]. – *Kāvyālaṁkāra* 5.34

The translator–annotator Sastry (1970: 93) comments:

> Here the colour steel-blue is attributed to the sky. . . . Similarly the action of coming from a distance is attributed to sounds. This kind of usage is permissible in *kāvya*. But this is all incorrect according to Śāstras. For, the sky has no colour . . . sound being the quality (of *ākāśa*, ether) cannot have action (*kriyā*) . . . and the great lights sun, moon, planets are not eternal.

And in Kāvya, *pratijñā* (proposition), is a statement of what one desires to postulate and not necessarily what is true or desirable. *Pratijñā* in Kāvya means a vow, and it can be founded in four causes – duty, worldly gain, love, anger. (For example, Bhīma vowing to drink his enemy's blood.) Such *pratijñā*s are then shown to be either fulfilled or violated, constituting elements of suspense, satisfaction or disconfirmation of expectation in the narrative. Thus Yudhiṣṭhira had resolved not to refuse to play dice if called upon to do so, and fulfils it by playing with Śakuni. Duryodhana, on the other hand, had resolved, after his defeat at the hands of the *gandharva*, Citrasena, to die by slow starvation, but came back for the sake of his kingdom. This is violation of *dharma* (Bhāmaha, *Kāvyālaṁkāra* 5.41).

These *pratijñās* (propositions or vows), become measures of the nobility or otherwise of characters in a *kāvya* for, as Bhāmaha tells us:

> Except in these four cases [duty, worldly gain, love, anger] vows should not be made. Once made, these four kinds should not be abandoned. – *Kāvyālaṁkāra* 5.40

Bhāmaha had begun this discussion by saying that only the unintelligent are afraid of the Śāstras. It is the proper function of *kāvya* to make the knowledge of Śāstras palatable. *Kāvya* does this by evoking *ānanda* or *rasa* as its central experience.

Text vs. Composition

This has to do with orality. In oral literatures, the compositions are open-ended – subject to accretions in every re-telling. The "texts" are closed – the readers may make many meanings out of them but their verbal content remains unchanged. India's texts such as *Mahābhārata*, on the other hand, are products of what may be called, "serial composition". We have Vālmīki *Rāmāyaṇa* and a thousand *Rāma-kathās*. There is Vyāsa's *Mahābhārata* and a thousand *Mahābhārata*-narratives across the length and breadth of this country. The pluralistic culture produces a plurality of texts. In the oral tradition, there is no one "authentic" text – all renditions and enunciations are "authentic". No reductionist attempt to prepare an "authentic" text is therefore valid.

4

Aesthetics of Literature and Reception

Aesthetics and Values

THERE is no opposition between aesthetics and ethics in Indian thought as all human endeavour in the Indian tradition must promote the four ends of life. Beauty (*saundarya*), the aesthetic parameter, is redefined as something, someone, some feeling or thought to which our mind attaches with reverence. What is the effect of the seated Buddha? It evokes an emotional state of deep tranquillity with accompanying joy (*ānanda*). Is that the goal of all art? If yes, what is its nature and how is it constituted? These and other questions are investigated in Indian poetics/aesthetics.

The aesthetic experience is a sacred experience. It is the cognition not of the appearance, of the perceptible forms, *prātibhāsika sattā*, but of *tattvārthika sattā*, the essence, *bhāva* of things. "Beauty" in art is not of the perceptible form but of the *bhāva* and all art therefore is an instrument of knowledge of essential reality and therefore is a means of education. Abhinavagupta at the very beginning of his commentary on *Nāṭyaśāstra* says that just as this unreal construction, called the world, through sensory inputs and meditation is the means of acquiring knowledge of the four ends of life (*puruṣārtha*), and of the ultimate end (*puruṣārtha*), the *śānta rasa*, in the same way this unstable, momentary and imaginary Rāma–Rāvaṇa business enacted by the *naṭa*, and manifesting wonderfully, is the instrument of knowledge of the four ends of life. Therefore, Abhinavagupta argues, the experiencer, the performer and the scholar of drama achieve the same result that the scholar of Veda does.

Verbal art, all art for that matter, is not an autonomous series – like all other human endeavours it must promote general human welfare. Therein lies its perennial value. "Aesthetics" as a science – a discipline – is the science of perceptible forms and accounts for nature, source, purpose and creative process of art, but its central concern is the nature and source of art experience. Traditionally, in the West, beauty has been the defining parameter of aesthetic experience though right from the beginning, from Plato to Ruskin, there have been voices that have argued a purpose, social or/and moral, of art experience. Aesthetics basically being the science of perceptible forms, India has not had a science (*śāstra*) of aesthetics. How can a cultural community that holds the object of perception, the appearance of things (*ābhāsa mātra*) as only a part, the ephemeral part, of the total reality develop a science of perceptible forms? Even Plato agrees that beauty, does not, cannot, belong to the appearance of things. In the West, this parameter of beauty has had a turbulent history particularly in the nineteenth and twentieth centuries – with Ruskin's moral imperative contending with Bentham's utility parameter. The aestheticist movement ended in the modernists, the great moderns with the aesthetic values becoming super-ordinate and replacing the religious/moral values. However, following the horrendous Second World War, faith in culture and such other systems of thought collapsed – to what end, it was asked, all the grand cultural achievements, this beauty and this grand faith? And the Western mind, the postmodernist mind reverted to ethics, to simple moral values and plurality of narratives.

Pre-eminence of beauty is in any case a recent position. Consider Plato's *Symposium*, Diotima's discourse in particular and the complex Greek value of beauty. Beauty is defined as appropriateness, the appropriateness of the object for its function. "Appropriateness" is then paraphrased as the power to perform its function, but this function may not always be productive of good. Is the power to produce evil also "beauty"? No. So beauty is generative of good, is goodness. In early nineteenth century, with the formation of egalitarian sociological thought, Bentham had, as we have already noted, argued within the British tradition that "usefulness" is the criterion of beauty while Ruskin counter-argued the moral principle as the criterion of beauty. So, in Western thought also, by and large, art has to have a purpose – utilitarian or moral, and, in recent times, social or political. In the nineteenth century, in the decades preceding First World War, for a brief while, we had the aestheticist movement of "art for art's sake". Plato's *Greater Hippias* is also a meditation on beauty. Beauty is that "by which all beautiful things are beautiful whether they appear so or not". So, beauty is autonomous of objects, and it is not something necessarily perceptible (cognizable by senses).

Plato reflects on the use of the word "beautiful" – "whatever is useful we call beautiful"; useful in the sense that it achieves the purpose for which it exists. (Strong legs, meant for running fast, are beautiful.) So that which has the power to achieve its purpose is beautiful. So power is a beautiful thing. But power without wisdom is ugly. So wisdom is beautiful. Plato from this, argues that "beauty is that which is both useful and powerful for some good purpose", i.e. "beauty is the cause of good".

Typically, at the end, Socrates casts a shadow of scepticism on all these positions – but, it is strongly suggested that beauty is a moral concept.

Now in Indian traditions of thought, "aesthetics" has not been a separate science (*vidyā*) and "beauty" (its construction) has not always been the goal of art, including verbal art. In fact, there is no opposition between "beauty" (aesthetics) and social/individual welfare (ethics) (a) in Indian art, including verbal art, and (b) in Indian theory of verbal art which includes in its domain both the *kavi* (poet) and the craftsman. It is possible to show that art in India has always been wedded to knowledge (*jñāna*) and therefore ethics (*puruṣārtha*). Examination of any one form of art – say narratives as verbal art – will show an evolution in the understanding of the goal of all art from promotion of personal ethics (*mokṣa*) to the establishment of public ethics (*lokasaṁgraha*).

Saundarya is not the overriding parameter of Indian art; though, it is the property that enables art to fulfil its goal (*lakṣaṇa* and *prayojana*). But it is not the defining property (locus, *ātmā*) of arts. Even as a property, it is not defined formally or in abstraction from the context of the artist, the object and the audience. Further, its nature (definition) is to be understood not only from theoretical discussions (by literary theorists in Kāvya Śāstra, for example) but also, and mainly, from the practice of verbal art (and other arts) by not only poets but also philosophers like Ādi Śaṅkara (in *Saundaryalaharī*, for example). From these, it will emerge that there is no opposition between "beauty" and "welfare", between aesthetics and ethics in Indian traditions of thought.

One must recognize that in the total Indian view, all human effort must serve the overriding ends of life, the *puruṣa-artha*s (*puruṣārtha*). The centrality of the *puruṣārtha* framework – *dharma*, *artha*, *kāma* and *mokṣa* in Indian life and thought cannot be overemphasized. There are various ways to understand this framework – as linear or as embedded structure. In this framework, *dharma* is the controlling category for the ensuing two, while *mokṣa* is the final goal. Art, therefore, also, is not an end in itself and, to be of any value, it must promote an understanding of how these ends have to be realized in individual and collective life.

Like all other worldly as well as spiritual pursuits, literature also is measured for its social and individual value by how it promotes the ends of life. Most Indian theorists are agreed on literature's purpose being promotion of the commonly accepted ends of life. Bharata at the very beginning in no uncertain terms asserted that literature is a discourse of knowledge – *pañcam veda,* a knowledge text as it mediates between philosophy and ordinary people who do actually need the ideas of philosophy but cannot access them. It ensures, he says,

> righteousness, good reputation, long life, well-being, increase in mental ability, and provides guidance to ordinary people in the conduct of life [and, also helps them] . . . have serious thoughts (*śāstrīyārtha*).

Bhāmaha, the next major thinker of sixth century CE, says that *kāvya* produces ability in *dharma, artha, kāma, mokṣa*. . . . He is so emphatic about literature being a rational discourse that, according to him, a non-philosopher cannot be a poet and a non-poet cannot be a philosopher. Daṇḍin, first half of seventh century CE, also says that apart from a natural endowment and practice, "knowledge of Śāstras" is an important component of a poet's ability. Vāmana (eighth/ninth century CE) said that *kāvya* being a cause (*hetu*) of *prīti*/*ānanda* is productive of visible/concrete worldly effect/fulfilment. Vāmana introduces this new idea of *ānanda* and only hints at how it relates to worldly fulfilment. Rudraṭa (eighth/ninth century CE) talks of "artful poets desirous of fulfilment of *puruṣārthas*. . . ." "Because," he continues, "this is the fulfilment of the knowledge of the knowledgeable ones, that their speech (language) matures through grammar and logic and results in attractive *kāvya*." This is important because "people are scared of dry philosophy (*nīrasa śāstra*) and easily achieve the four *puruṣārthas* (*caturavarga*) through *kāvya*".

From Bharata to Rudraṭa it is clear that verbal art is closely related to life of the people – as oral literature, aural–visual in character, it is specifically able to disseminate knowledge widely. What knowledge? Kṣemendra says:

> What is the use of *alaṁkara* and vain enumeration of *guṇa* for literary compositions so long as no one, even after considerable effort, gains from them life-appropriateness (*jīvana-aucitya*)?

Literature in our tradition is *dṛṣṭānta* for all Śāstras – *dharma, artha, kāma* and *mokṣa*.

Bhojarāja formulated his theory that *śṛṅgāra* is the source-*rasa*, the primary state of being. From eighth century to the eleventh century, we see in Indian art a movement that sees the growing predominance of *śṛṅgāra* and *rati.*

This is the period of great temple architecture and Khajurāho, the Orissa sculptures. This and the gradual strengthening of Śakti and Śākta (Tantra) systems led to a focus on the female form as an object of adoration. Some of the most beautiful sculptures are of the goddesses Pārvatī, Lakṣmī and Sarasvatī embellished with all the *guṇa* and *alaṁkāra*. In this perspective, Ādi Śaṅkara's *Saundaryalaharī* is a very significant composition. It is conventionally divided into two parts – the first forty-one verses constitute *Ānandalaharī*, dealing as they do with matters of intellect and spirit. The next fifty-nine verses constitute *Saundaryalaharī* where each verse is devoted to one aspect of the beauty of form of Tripurasundarī. Śaṅkara's great achievement is how faced with extreme physical, bodily beauty, he transmutes the lust of the observer into devotion, turns the observer into a devotee, a *sādhaka*. The object is for once an object of beauty; it is evoked beautifully but the effect is not *śṛṅgāra* but *śānta* which later in

Abhinavagupta's theory becomes the source state of being, and all *tapas* is subordinated to this end.

Even crafting of beauty is a *tapas* and the artist who crafts it is a *sādhaka*, a *yogī* and there is no hiatus between the mundane and the divine. The creative process is the process of giving *rūpa* to *dravya* and is a form of *yoga* (meditation). The mind of the artist attaches to the object of adoration with reverence and that object becomes beautiful. The paradigm artist/craftsman is the potter (*kumbhakāra*) who does not, unlike the carpenter, measure, segment or rearrange but merely makes manifest what already exists – as a *krāntadarśina*, one who dwells in the higher reaches of the mind. His function is to make us see what he has seen. The potter's art is socially relevant and the *ghaṭa* (pitcher) he makes is a profound philosophical symbol (*ghaṭākāśa*) and also a very important element in the religious and social ritual, and life of the Indian people.

After the contact with the West through English literature, we started talking of "Saundaryaśāstra" as an autonomous subject and *saundarya* became a subject of discussion under the influence of Croce initially (Gulab Rai 1944, 2020 Vikramī Saṁvat) and ending up with Marxism (Ram Bilas Sharma 1911). The discussion begins around: (a) what is beauty? (b) where does it reside? (c) is it universally definable or is it in particulars?

One need not go into what all the twentieth-century poets and poeticians have said on these questions – the answers fall into predictable routines. Instead, we take note of the fact that in the process, under the influence of Western thought, an opposition was set up between art and morality, aesthetics and ethics in India as well.

What Shyam Sundardas had to say about this in the 1930s is still sufficiently explanatory. As mankind advanced into civil society, the knowledge of right and wrong became stronger, and ethics became virtually a part of human nature. Man's discriminating intellect exercises a control on his desires and his emotional/mental status grows mature through reflection. Arts, informed by thus matured/refined mental/emotional states, are reflections of the right/good cognitions (*sadvṛttīya*) of that society. The more cultured a community or state is, the more "beautiful", "constructive"/positive its artefacts shall be. So ethics has an important place in all art.

But some Western scholars have come up with some counter-positions. The fourfold *puruṣārtha* structure which then functions as the goal of all human efforts, including art.

(a) The psychologists argue that the emotions that are suppressed by culture and society find expression in art. If this is accepted, ethics must quit art. But there are manifest exceptions to this principle. The portraits of a beautiful woman or an effulgent *saṁnyāsī* will not be fruitfully analysed through the motivations of the artists. One fact is self-evident, the greatest works of art in human history have been the products of highly discriminating ethical individuals.

(b) The second argument is of the "realists", broadly who say that the basic tendencies of man are for the fulfilment of his basic needs and that the "noble" tendencies (*udāttavṛtti*s) are superficial and secondary and serve only cultural needs. Indian thinkers have constantly opposed this. The need to build on a long-evolving culture is the reason for practising good conduct. Even the animals are not treated at the level of body or physical needs alone. (Animals are not objects of disgust or fear; *avatāra*s take animal form; animals are human, gods, *vāhana,* etc.; animal figures are correct in temples.)

(c) The third counter-position adopted for a period of time is that of aesthetics – "art for art's sake". This is

> the spiritual forerunner of the aesthetic salvation sought by the great moderns.

It is true that art objects are studied in themselves and compared for realization of the parameters that emerge from the practice of that art and in that evaluation. The question of ethical purpose is irrelevant. There are rules of crafting and rules of expression that are independent of rules of other systems – you can't have, for example, a *nirguṇa* sculpture. But this does not mean that art as an activity as a whole does not have anything to do with ethics. The more democratic an art is, the more effect it has on people, and a cultured, civil society will have expectations from art, as it has from bridge-building technology, for example. This is what Plato was saying when he said that the presence of Homer had contributed nothing towards improving the conduct of the people. Art can have, does have, a social role, a philosophical role, an ethical role – it will be determined by the community within which it functions. But how well that role is performed will be determined by how well the art object has been crafted and, therefore, how many people willingly seek to experience it. In this the "metropolitan" derivative art of India must be contrasted with the traditional, popular *śravya-prekṣā* art of the "other", in its democratic nature, unlimited audience, wide reach, sources in tradition, thought and culture and deep, abiding effect that a poet such as Tulsī or Kabīr has had on Indian masses.

Reception

How is art experience received and what are the processes of reception? How does *rasabodha* (cognition or knowledge of *rasa*) take place? What cognitive process/processes are involved and what is the nature of this experience, this *rasabodha* or *rasānubhūti* (experience of *rasa*)? How does it lead to or result in *ānanda*?

Bharata's *rasa siddhānta* claims that there are eight basic *sthāyī bhāvas*, relatively durable states of being. These *sthāyī bhāvas* are of the nature of *cittavṛttis*, cognitive processes of the self brought about by *vibhāvas*, the causal factors. *Anubhāvas* the physical manifestations, are reflexes of these core *cittavrttis* – the *sthāyī bhāvas*. The ancillary states of being, the *sañcārī bhāvas*, reinforce the basic eight *sthāyī bhāvas*. It is the primary *cittavrtti bhāvas* that get constituted as *rasa* experience.

Now these *vṛttis* exist in the consciousness, the *antaḥkaraṇa*, the knowing self, the cognitive system. This cognitive system has four parts or functional modules or divisions – *indriya*, *mana*, *buddhi* and *citta*. The system constitutes *ahaṁkāra*, the *ākāra* (form) that the self, *aham*, takes. These have been succinctly described by Ādi Śaṅkara, who says:

> Decisiveness and predication (*saṅkalpa-vikalpa*) are the *dharma* (intrinsic property) of *mana* (mind); determining the objects (*padārtha*) with certainty of *buddhi* (intellect); myself, myself this awareness of *ahaṁkāra*; and reflection on its own properties of *citta*. – *Vivekacūḍāmaṇi*, *kārikās* 95-96

Mana is like the master switch, an instrument, of a static circuit – a structure with a circuit. It is "switched on" for cognition and then the circuit becomes operational and when it is tuned to the right frequency, it starts receiving signals (impressions). The capacity of the circuit to process the signals and recognize them is the function of the intellect (*buddhi*). *Mana* has the ability to receive impressions, *buddhi* is the system that analyses them, categorizes them. Once so recognized, the impressions impress themselves on *citta* – like the first raindrops on dry earth. *Citta* absorbs experience and it becomes "holed", i.e. marked, like a loaf of bread. Such burdened/loaded *citta*, a cause of distraction, is the structured self. According to one school of thought, *citta* has two properties – it is self-aware (*prakāśamaya*) and it has the ability to permute its knowledge (*vimarśa*) to combine, to rearrange, to create new understandings from available information. It interprets, and the new understanding that emerges becomes a part of our being.

The subsequent theorists have elaborated the process and asked two questions:

1. The *rasa* we experience, where or in what does it exist? What is the substratum of the *rasa* we experience and enjoy?
2. What is the nature of this knowledge (of *rasa*), this *rasātmaka bodha*? Is this literary knowledge a knowledge based in perception or in inference or in *śabda* (word)?

Four major commentators are reported in the tradition to have answered these questions (see Kapil Kapoor and Nalini Ratnam 1998 pp. 111-15).

The first interpretation is given by Lollaṭa Bhaṭṭa and his followers; the emotion that a viewer experiences, though primarily and really subsisting in the character personated, e.g. Rāma, comes to be recognized as subsisting in the personating actor by reason of his having assumed that character and when thus recognized, it is called *rasa*. Jha (1925: 49) comments on this thus:

> This theory is open to the objection that it fails to explain the emotion that arises in the mind of the spectator of the dramatic representation; as according to it, the sentiment is generated in the *personated* character and secondarily recognized in the personating character.

In Śaṅkuka's interpretation,

> the *saṁyoga* of *vibhāva, anubhāva* and *sañcārī bhāva* leads to the inference of the latent emotion of love . . . the emotion by

> reason of the peculiar charm, different from all other objects of inference, and hence it is recognized . . . as something relished (*āsvādita*)] . . . it is imagined to be subsisting latently in the actor; and even though not really present in him, it is relished by the spectators through their predisposed tendencies. – Jha 1925: 51

Jha (1925: 51) comments on this position thus:

> Under this view, the causes, effects and auxiliaries are the inevitable concomitants of the emotion – and hence when they are perceived, in the actor, they lead to the inference of the emotion; and the inference of this non-existent emotion is explained as being due to the predisposition of the audience.
>
> The objection against this view is that inference is a purely intellectual process, and hence cannot account for the highly complex emotional phenomena involved in *rasa*.

The third interpretation, that of Bhaṭṭanāyaka, is interesting for its innovativeness – *rasa* is not cognized (inferred) or generated or manifested, either unconcernedly (as not concerning the spectator at all, as held by Lollaṭa Bhaṭṭa) or as subsisting in the spectator himself (relished by him, as Śaṅkuka believes). As a matter of fact, in poetry and drama, words are invested with a peculiar power or potency (*bhāvanā*) – different from direct denotation (*abhidhā*) and indirect indication (*lakṣaṇā*) – which generates the *vibhāvas*, *anubhāvas* and *sañcārī bhāvas*, and thereby presents to consciousness the "latent emotion" (*bhāva*) which then comes to be relished (experienced) by a process of delectation abounding in enlightenment and bliss due to the plenitude of the quality of harmony (*sattva*).[1] Jha (1925: 51) comments on this:

---

1 *sattvodreka prakāśānandamayasaṁvidā viśrānti satattvena bhogena bhujyate iti bhaṭṭanāyaka* – Mammaṭa, *Kāvyaprakāśa*, chapter 4.

> According to this view the relishing (*āsvādana*) of *rasa* is the outcome of the purely verbal process of generalized presentation (*sādhāraṇīkaraṇa*). This is open to the objection that it makes the unwarranted assumption of this last mentioned verbal process.

Mammaṭa explains the fourth interpretation, that of Abhinavagupta, the now standard interpretation of *rasa* experience. An important aspect of Abhinavagupta's thinking is that he extends the *rasa* theory to all compositions; in fact his arguments make it a general theory of art. *Cittavṛtti*s (the *sthāyī bhāva*s) are inherent as predispositions. They become manifest (*vyakta*) when they come in contact with pertinent experience which becomes generalized in a literary representation. The viewer's separate personality weakens and his consciousness merges in the universal experience and he experiences *rasa*. This *rasa* exists only in this apprehension and once manifest produces *alaukika ānanda* (transcendent charm). Though it exists only in the *āsvadāna* (relish), it may be regarded as something to be known, to be cognized (*jñāpya*) as it forms the object of a super-physical consciousness and as such differs from perception and other ordinary forms of cognition. Abhinavagupta's position differs from Bhaṭṭanāyaka's in that the *bhāva* is present in the mind of the spectator in the form of a predisposition.

Consider Abhinavagupta's position in a little more detail. According to this, a man in his lifetime experiences a number of *bhāva*s at different times – he loves someone, worries about someone, is angry at someone, or disgusted with someone, or afraid of someone, laughs at someone or is overawed by someone. At times, though rarely, he experiences total peace. These experiences come and go but their traces, the impressions become part of his heart/mind in the form of *saṁskāra*s. These *bhāva*s that exist in the human heart in the form of *vāsanā*s (*vāsanā*, that which permeates the self) are the *sthāyī bhāva*s of literature. The *sthāyī bhāva*s thus are tendencies or dispositions – *cittavṛttis*. When we (re)cognize these *bhāva*s by means of enlightened bliss in the self (*prakāśamaya ātmānanda*), the very same *bhāva*s are designated as *rasa*. "Enlightened" because the *citta* is self-aware – we become aware of our own self in the acute emotional experience and also because this experience of *ānanda* is an enrichment of our being/sensibility as at that moment and in that moment we are endowed with the ability to feel the suffering, etc. of the other, of someone else, as our own. For the moment, we are transformed and are nobler than our real self.

When does this happen – this cognition of *bhāva*s as bliss? It happens only when we are sufficiently educated in our feelings, i.e. when our self is rid of the layer of ignorance (*ajñāna*). So though grief is a latent predisposition in all, not all may graduate to compassion. How is this layer of ignorance removed – by the process of *sādhāraṇīkaraṇa*, i.e. a comprehension of the general nature of a *bhāva*, such as grief, from particular instances independent of the specific objects and events involved. It is then experienced as the experience of the self. The self-aware consciousness (that is consciousness in the form of the self), when rid of ignorance and, being of the nature of qualities of *antaḥkaraṇa* (*mana–buddhi–citta* structure), enlightens the *sthāyī bhāva*s inherent in *vibhāva*s, etc. and being inseparable from the *bhāva*s, becomes the object of relish (*rasānanda*).

What is the nature of this cognition of *bhāva* by *ātmacaitanya* (self in the form of consciousness/intellect)? There are two kinds of cognitions – the cognition of external objects such as *ghaṭa* (pot), *paṭa* (curtain) and the cognition of *bhāva*s internal to the cognizing self. In the first, the cognitive apparatus (*antaḥkaraṇa*, i.e. *mana*, *buddhi* and *citta*) is required. In the second, the objects of cognition, which are among the qualities/ properties of the self, become illumined for us to experience them. The first cognition is like the cognition of a horse in our wakeful state; the second is like the cognition of a horse-in dream, which is *sākṣībhāṣya,* i.e. made cognizable by the consciousness itself.

If *rasa* is an inherent property of the self, why do we not constantly experience it and why does everyone not experience it to the same degree? That is, what are the necessary/ sufficient conditions of aesthetic realization? The answers are implicit in the above process. It is when the experience – *vibhāvas*, etc. – has been truly and completely internalized that *bhāva* is experienced as *rasa* and second, what is needed is *sahṛdayatā* which makes it possible to grasp the true (general) nature (*bhāvanā*) of a literary experience. On account of that, the quality of relish of generalized *vibhāvas* is determined by the degree of *sahṛdayatā* and in cases of total empathy, the self takes the form of *ānanda* and the viewer is immersed in this. This state is *rasānubhūti.*

What is the nature of this *ānanda*? Since its ultimate source is in worldly experience, it is *laukika,* not spiritual (*brahmānanda*), not something totally delinked from objects, yet it is not like other-worldly pleasures in which the cognitive mechanism, including the senses, is directly involved. In the case of literary experience, the *citta* itself is transformed into *ānanda* (bliss or happiness). So *kāvyānanda* is different from both *viṣayānanda* and *brahmānanda.* This *rasa* experience may be characterized as an intellectual cognition, i.e. consciousness modified by an awareness of the *bhāva* or the *bhāva* qualified by consciousness. In this *rasāsvāda,* the relish of the emotional state, there is *sukha* (a synonym for *harṣa* (joy) *vide Amarakośa* 1.4.25). There is joy in every *bhāva* even in *śoka* (deep grief). There are two sorts of evidence for this – (1) the Śruti (*raso vai saḥ*), and (2) our knowledge of how people respond to art enactments. Thus happenings like separation from a loved one produce grief in the material world but its representation in a poem or a painting or a frieze becomes *alaukika* (supranormal) in a literary enactment. So just as *śṛṅgāra rasa* compositions give *sukha,* the *karuṇa rasa* compositions too do the same. The tears that flow from witnessing divinity, kindness or sorrow are indicative of *ānanda.* "All these (*bhāvas*) being self-manifesting and relished cognitions, being permeated with *ānanda,* are predominantly sources of *sukha*" (Abhinavagupta on *Nāṭyaśāstra* 6.31).

What is the status of this literary enjoyment, *ānanda*? It is said to be different from both *viṣayānanda* (*pravṛtti*) and *brahmānanda* (*nivṛtti*), though some claim that *bhakti rasa* comes closest to *brahmānanda,* while others claim that it is *laukika* (material) and the physical process is the same. Notice that we are all deeply moved and moved often to *karuṇa rasa* even in the moments of devotion. For example, Lord Kṛṣṇa asking Draupadī for a shred of cloth to bind his bleeding little finger – the Lord who had invested her with yards and yards to protect her modesty – and Draupadī now with tears in her eyes for the Lord's infinite mercy, vowing to tear the border of her priceless wedding *sāṛī* – we the *sahṛdaya,* are moved to tears.

How do we explain these tears? We humans are naturally selfish, aware only of our own afflictions, real or imaginary. And yet we amazingly cry over the suffering of the other! We have to account for this effect of *rasānubhūti* (the art experience). We are moved to tears at the suffering of the other – so, for the moment, as we have said, we have become nobler than we actually are in life, larger than our small self. Thus we transcend our narrow self through art experience. For the moment we have gained *mokṣa,* are liberated as we have felt the suffering of others as our own. Viśvanātha says in the presence of great art, the *sattva* predominates and we have *āhlāda/ānanda,* this melting or softening or liquefaction of our psyche,

> unified by predominance of *sattva*, self-illuminating, joy-permeated, in the form of knowledge, unconnected with objects, virtually like witnessing Brahmā, a formless reality"
>
> – *Sāhitya-Darpaṇa* 3.2-3

This is the value of art – it educates us in human values by "moving" us, by transforming our inner self.

5

Philosophy of Literature

Two assertions, or claims, about literature *(kāvya)* are made in the tradition. First that knowledge contained in learned texts is dry, tedious and difficult to access. But when it is communicated through a poem, a story or a play, it becomes joyful (*sārasa*), simple (*sarala*) and compehensible. Therefore, Abhinavagupta says that just as medicine mixed in milk becomes palatable, difficult and dry knowledge becomes palatable in literature. The second major assertion is that art transforms the self of the experiencers and morally uplifts them. It is for these two reasons that great compositions, such as the two epics, hava a perennial charm and value for the ordinary Indians.

We have already indicated that all art, indeed all knowledge, in India's intellectual traditions, we had noted,[1] is inflected by values. Knowledge must promote *dharma* (righteousness) by inculcating *sadvr̥ttis* (affirmative thought currents or values). The architecture of the temples, the *vāstu* of dwellings and the practices of Buddhist *vihāra* are concrete expressions of *saḍvr̥ttis*, the positive values that are the determinants of *r̥ta*, the equilibrium that is the condition of all

---

1 See Kapil Kapoor, "Aesthetics and Values", in R. Balasubramanian (ed.) *The Enworlded Subjectivity: Its Three Worlds and Beyond*, in History of Science, Philosophy and Culture, Volume IX, New Delhi: Centre for Studies in Civilization, 2006, pp. 654-74.

existence – individual, societal and cosmic. The centrality of the *puruṣārtha* framework – *dharma, artha, kāma* and *mokṣa* – in Indian life and thought cannot be overemphasized. All art, like all worthy human endeavour, must foster *dharma,* the first and the foremost of the universally acknowledged four ends of life – the *puruṣārtha.* Like other worldly as well as spiritual pursuits, even the verbal art,[2] is to be measured for its social and individual value, by what ends of life it promotes and how well. Bharata says that verbal art is a knowledge text because it mediates between philosophy and ordinary people, and primarily ensures righteousness: "righteousness, good reputation, long life, well-being, increase in mental ability" and provides "guidance to ordinary in the conduct of life [and also helps them] . . . have serious thoughts (*śāstrīyārtha*)".[3]

In that perspective, the literary theorists say that for each of the four ends, a Śāstra exists – Dharmaśāstra for *dharma,* Arthaśāstra for *artha,* Kāmaśāstra for *kāma* and Mokṣaśāstra for *mokṣa.* This being the case, the literary theorists ask what function Kāvya (literature) serves. The tradition says that literature serves as a *dṛṣṭānta* (illustration/exemplar) for all the four. That is, literature illustrates the basic concepts of all the four Śāstras through narratives of particular individuals and events that are typical examples of adherence or violation of those concepts. That also explains why Bharata calls *nāṭya,* the fifth Veda. It mediates between ordinary people and the knowledge texts such as Vedas and Upaniṣads.

Most Indian theorists are agreed on literature's purpose being the promotion of commonly accepted ends of life. Bharata at the very beginning in no uncertain terms asserts

---

2 Substantial thinking about aesthetics has taken place in India with reference to the verbal art and what the literary theorists have thought and said about verbal art applies generally to all arts.

3 *Nāṭyaśāstra* I.14-15.

that literature is a discourse of knowledge – *pañcam veda* – a knowledge text.

The art experience therefore is perceived as a transforming experience as the *ānanda* (joy) experienced is illuminating, enlightening, liberating – the experiencer acquires new, affirmative cognitions and thereby escapes from his narrow self and his inherent worldly tendencies and becomes nobler than he actually may be. It is *sattvodreka prakāśamaya*, the ascendance of purity and the consequent effulgence, as Abhinavagupta says. We have to account for this effect of art experience. For example, in a sad narative/representation, we are moved to tears at the suffering of the other, say Daśaratha's grief at his separation from his son, and for the moment, as we have noted, we become nobler than we actually are in life, larger than our small self. Thus we transcend our narrow self through art experience. For the moment we have gained *mokṣa,* are liberated as we have felt the suffering of others as our own. Viśvanātha says in the presence of great art, the *sattva* predominates and we have *āhlāda/ānanda,* this melting or softening or liquefaction of our psyche: "unified by predominance of *sattva,* self-illuminating, joy-permeated, in the form of knowledge, unconnected with objects, virtually like witnessing Brahmā, a formless reality" (*Sāhitya-Darpaṇa* 3.2-3).

What is it that moves us deeply enough to change us? It is evidently an experience that brings out the noble or the need for the noble, in man; it moves us because it makes an appeal to some of the noblest human emotions. It is an experience that borders on sacred.

A man in his lifetime experiences a number of *bhāva*s at different times – he loves someone, worries about someone, is angry at someone, or disgusted with someone, or afraid of someone, laughs at someone or is overawed by someone. At times, though rarely, he experiences total peace. These experiences come and go but their traces, the impressions become part of his heart/mind in the form of *saṁskāras*. These *bhāvas* that exist in the human hearts in the form of *vāsanās* (*vāsanā*, that which permeates the self) that are the *sthāyī bhāvas* of literature. The *sthāyī bhāvas* thus are tendencies or dispositions (*cittavṛttis*). When we (re)cognize these *bhāvas* by means of enlightened bliss in the self (*prakāśamaya ātmānanda*), the very same *bhāvas* are designated as *rasa*. In an art experience because the *citta* becomes self-aware – we become aware of our own self in the acute emotional experience and also because this experience of *ānanda* is an enrichment of our being/sensibility as at that moment and in that moment we are endowed with the ability to feel the suffering, etc. of the other, of someone else, as our own. For the moment, we are transformed and are nobler than our real self.

Therefore *kāvya*, literature is perceived to have, is assigned a pervasive role in Indian society. Literature is a community experience, individuals do read *kāvya* either as a ritual *pāṭha* or for *adhyayana*, scholarly study. But the most widespread reception of *kāvya*, literature, is through social participation. This "social participation" takes many forms. A large body of compositions in India is performative in character – these compositions are narrated, performed or collectively enacted before a large, diverse audience. The *kathā paramparā* and the folk-performance *paramparā* are completely democratic. They are held in the open, there is no ticket, and all and everybody can join, sit, listen, see and leave when he/she wants to. It is this social dimension of literature that has made literature a disseminator of knowledge, the *pañcama veda* that mediates between the masses and the knowledge texts. If the average Indian is highly "educated", though he may not be "literate", it is because of the widespread social participative function of literatures of all Indian languages.

And this would not have been possible if Indian literature was scriptal, written, in its basic mode. In fact, India's oral culture has generated the vast body of Indian literatures that are essentially oral. Orality of Indian literatures also determines the characteristic aural-visual forms.

This phonocentrism of the Indian mind was perhaps the result as well as the reinforcing factor of the orality of Indian culture. Orality is an alternative culture – it may get written down or may co-exist with written analogue or it may not get written down. But even when an oral culture gets written down, it continues to be oral – witness for example texts such as *Mahābhārata* that remain recitative, performative texts even when rendered in different languages.

Given this, there is need for perspective shift in our study of Indian literatures. First of all oral compositions are total audio-visual experience; in the written version audio and prosodic features as well as features of performance go absent. Oral compositions are de-contextualized, anonymous, structurally baggy, hierarchic (narratives/lyrics within narratives/lyrics), metrical, open to innovation and extension (even in the act of rendering). They are closely interwoven with the life of the community. In a society where reverence for the uttered word is deep, the distinction between the oral culture and literature becomes untenable. In fact, the oral culture becomes the literature of that people. Oral language being dialogic and written language being monologic, oral literature is necessarily participative with people participating in the performance/rendering. The direct and immediate visual and auditory participation in the act of oral communication presupposes high degree of interaction between living persons physically present in the communication link, whereas in the more intellectual and abstract context of written language addressed to an absent or an imaginary receiver, such intimacy is more certainly lost.

It is to be noted that more and more oral literatures of India are getting written down to "maintain"the oral compositions that are increasingly dying in the onslaught of seriptal, material culture that is spreading as part of the main stream education syestem. But when the oral compositions get written down, their oral features are lost and when they get "videod", many dimensions of the live performance are lost. Therefore what is "maintained"is only a small part of the original. The danger is that oral culture is universally lost.

Oral literature is truly democratic – it has the whole community as its audience and it requires no special ability or skill, such as reading, for its reception.

Understandably, therefore, we need a different vocabulary to discuss this oral literature. In place of *author, reader,* and *text,* we need to use terms such as *composer, auditor,* and *composition* for obvious reasons. Also we need to abjure the use of words such as *primitive, tribal.*

For a comprehensive Indian theory of literature, we need to work out the parameters for analysis of oral literatures. For each composition, we have to consider:

1. theme/content
2. occasion of performance
3. medium – verse/prose
4. participation/participants
5. structure – metre, number of lines (in case of poems), organization (stanzas), length, rhyme scheme, rhymes, prosodic features (like assonance)
6. +/– performative
7. mode of composition
8. composer(s) – male/female
9. community specificity

10. rendering frame
11. re-telling/fresh composition.

Each of these has to be analysed and must categories need to be formulated.

Evidently, many of these parameters are specific to oral literatures.

Some questions also need to be addressed. These questions rise out of the flux and variability and consequent possibility of loss of oral compositions. Some of these involve deliberations about:

1. the evaluation of ethnographic approach to literature
2. use of concepts such as "tribal (communities)" and their assumptions
3. the possibilities of ". . . compositions surviving (?) in oral form . . ."
4. the question of "dialect" of a given literary language . . . or an independent language
5. writing as an adequate means of recording literary compositions
6. technological recording and the nature of oral compositions
7. translations into English and/or other Indian languages as "maintaining" device.

In sum, the following major issues are crucial:

1. Approach and assumptions: cultural-synthesizing (questions/motivations – identity vs. belonging)
2. literary terminology, concepts or constructs
3. "safeguarding" (?) orality – means and modes
4. translatability and translations problems such as retaining rhymes and metres and/or other "orality" features

5. new audio-visual technologies and dissemination of increased access.

The aesthetics of Indian literatures is essentially the aesthetics of an oral, performative experience. This "aesthetics" appeals to all the senses, the mind and the heart.

Experience shapes us and art, as surrogate experience shapes us more effectively by virtue of its aesthetic mode, its appeal of beauty. But what is beauty? What is its place/role in art? Abhinavagupta reserves the term *saundarya* for crafting the discourse – for only when so crafted does it delight and also generate new knowledge or awareness in the auditor – a discourse

> that acquires beauty (*sundaratā*) through *guṇa, alaṁkāra, aucitya. . . .*[4]

Beauty (*saundarya*) therefore is merely instrumental in the fulfilment of the primary goal of verbal art – it is not the end. *Saundarya* is quite a simple system:

What is the content of *saundarya*? The answers differ from one culture to another and produce differences in the aesthetics of communities. The answers depend on the purposes of art in a society apart from the philosophy and the world-view of a

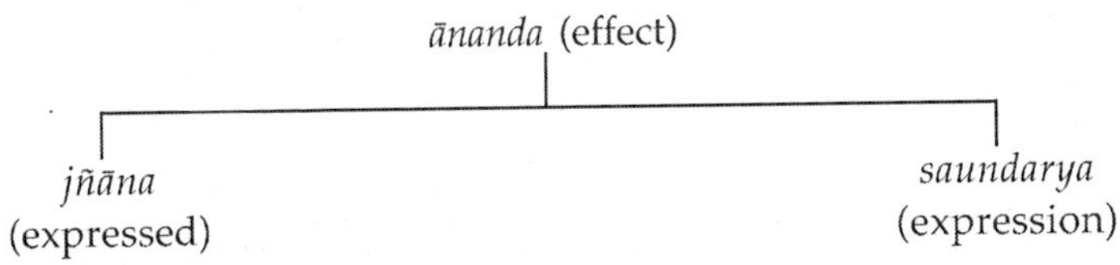

community. In Indian theories of art and literature, the states of mind, emotional states constitute the core aesthetic experience – art creates and communicates these states of mind, these dominant emotional states, and the reader/viewer/audience

---

[4] *guṇa alaṁkāra aucitya sundaraśabdārthaśarīrasya . . .*

experiences these states of mind. If the art/literary compositions succeed in giving enjoyment by evoking some state(s) of mind, then the work is aesthetically satisfactory. Beauty in fact is secondary – the evocation and communication of a state of mind is judged successful if it moves the reader/hearer and affects him deeply, in which case the work of art is beautiful.

Beautiful is what moves the people, affects them deeply, is determined as we have said above by their world-view, their philosophy of life. Cultural differences of various communities show in their respective aesthetics, in the kind of emotional/intellectual content that is claimed to have more beauty, i.e. greater capacity, to move or affect the audience. It may be safely said that in Indian aesthetics this emotion is compassion (*karuṇa*), the selflessness of the human heart. Compassion and tranquillity (at peace with oneself) are the two core elements of beauty in Indian art/literature. These are the co-ordinates of Abhinavagupta's *śānta rasa*. Witness, for example, the detached, contemplative, inward-oriented, Gandhāra seated Buddha.

For the Indian mind, whatever moves us deeply is "beautiful". Anything to which our mind attaches with reverence is "beautiful". Aesthetics is determined by the world-view of a people, we said. The Indian world-view upholds certain values, the *daivī sampadā* of *Bhagavad-Gītā* and/or the *sadvṛttis* of *Caraka Saṁhitā*. What are these values dear to the Indian mind? In Indian aesthetics, *selflessness* is beauty – human goodness, not necessarily ethical rightness, but a goodness of feeling and instincts. Beauty consists in the inherent harmony, and all action is directed towards restoration of this harmony or balance (order), which is achieved when the *āsurī vṛttis* are subdued by *daivī vṛttis*. This cosmic view with its implications for man's non-individuality – interlinking rather than discreteness of single objects, every being subordinate to the universal order, imposes restrictions on the Indian artist. First, there is the absence of biography – the fact of anonymity of the artist/craftsman. This because single personalities have no importance in the cosmic frame – there is no individual meaning, no authorial intent. Second, there is no self-expression – there is no literature of self-expression dealing with the traumas and dilemmas of the artist or the individual. In fact, there is no free choice of the subject – there is constant renewal and reinterpretation of the classical narratives and themes. Novelty is not the aim – it is a deeper understanding of the experience that the succeeding artists aim at.

Art is never a discipline purely in itself – there are no uniquely aesthetic goals. So the artist takes themes from other areas – Itihāsa and Purāṇas, and Śrutis. Hence like all knowledge, art too is subservient to *dharma,* which is the ultimate justification for all human endeavour. It is not accidental that ancient India made in stone only temples and images of gods and goddesses – not public buildings. The symbolism – including geometric designs in temple architecture, handicrafts and arts – reflects these fundamental beliefs, and is the real value of art, rather than its usefulness. Thus, for example, it has been pointed out, the richness of tropical nature as captured in the minute and varied carvings in architecture and in the profuse imagery, the garlands of similes (*mālopama*) in literary compositions, has its origin in nature in a major way. At the same time, there is a continuity between the inanimate and the animate, and between the animate and the divine. So we have the world's finest animal fables in which what is said about the animals is true of every being including gods and men. We do not have horror-animals – animals that frighten. When there is such an object – a horrifying animal – as, for example, the Bakāsura in Lord Kṛṣṇa's childhood tales (*bāla-līlā*), it is generally men, or *asura*s who take that form. And our gods take animal form too – the *matsya* and *varāha avatāra*s. And the gods often take half-animal, half-human forms – Gaṇeśa and Narasiṁha, for example.

All this shows deep respect for all life and a rejection of man's predominant status. This itself is a value of much significance for human life. This is also a part of how all existence tends towards identification with the universal spirit and we recognize that the pervasive theme of love in epics, plays and lyrical poetry is an expression of this idea. The repetition of forms and themes (in sculpture, architecture and poetry), the predominance of grouped forms rather than individual, and the sculpturing of figures in mountain or hill-sides or in the jungles reflect both the plurality of being and the final absorption of individual existence in the universal being. All this is an attempted re-creation of the *epic* of life – the mysterious, multiple, marvellous reality that invites, and allows, only contemplation of an image or idol-making (which is a kind of reproduction). The magnificent range, variety and detail of the *Mahābhārata* are an attempted reproduction, an image of the range, variety and detail of the universe. And the seated Buddha – divine and contemplative – is the paradigm image of this world-view.

Two constructs constitute the substantial world-view of the average Indian and control his attitude to life, his conduct and art. The popular understanding of the Vedāntic ontological claim that this whole universe is made up of pulsating matter *and* that the objects we cognize around us are simply forms that rise in and collapse back into the pulsating matter. All these forms are transient and the energized matter is the enduring reality. For example, the wave, the bubbles and the froth are forms that we see on the surface of river-water but they come and go and the river-water flows on. This is a very dynamic view of reality as changeful and changing all the time, one that frees man from "attachment" to what are after all mere forms. Hence the Indian art's concern with not just the perceptible but with the reality beyond the perceptible.

This leads to the second major construct that shapes the common Indian's world-view. As man is just one of the innumerable "forms", what is his status in relation to other forms in this universe? Here, we arrive at an understanding fundamentally at variance with the Hebraic world-view and one that renders the Indian world-view as basically ethical.

In the Hebraic–Christian world-view, man is at the centre of the creation. Made in His own image, God invites him to exercise dominion over all the creation.[5] With this sanction, the Western man has felt entitled to exploit the resources, bending nature to man's purpose, so that, today, an ecological disaster confronts mankind. Add to this the monistic imperative – one God and that too my God, *not* your God – and we have the ready structure of a *conflict model* based on opposition, exploitation and subjection, a model that generates and promotes *adversarial* relations between man and God (a punishing or an angry God), man and nature (nature to be modified to ensure man's comfort), between man and man (Marxism) and now between man and woman (gender theory). As against this, Indian philosophic thought structures a harmony model based on unity, welfare and freedom of all beings. Man in the Indian world-view is just one link in the Chain of Being (1,84,000 *yoni*s (units or beings) in the life-cycle). The world has not been created for him alone and he has only as much claim on its resources as any other creature. As the same life principle informs all beings, all are equal; since the same spirit abides in all, there is no enemy and no

---

[5] "And God said, Let us make man in our own image after our likeness: and let him have dominion over the fish of the sea and over the fowl of the air, and over the cattle, and over all the earth and over every creeping thing that creepeth upon the earth."
– Genesis 1: 26

room for enmity. The *Bhagavad-Gītā* succinctly and explicitly lays down this doctrine of unity of all beings in the following sequence of verses in chapter VI:

> . . . united in identity with all-pervading infinite consciousness . . . sees unity everywhere, beholds the self present in all beings. . . . – verse 29
>
> He who sees Me (the Universal Self) present in all beings, and all beings existing within Me. . . . – verse 30
>
> He who looks on all as one, on the analogy of his own self, and looks upon the joy and sorrow of all with a similar eye. . . . – verse 32

This foundational idea determines the values that are upheld in Indian life and in art – *sadvṛttis* (positive or affirmative cognitions) of the Yoga system. Good *vṛttis* have a restorative and curative value. Aristotle at the source of Western aesthetics had argued the restorative value of art – *catharsis*.[6] Bharata about the same time explained that drama as an art form was introduced to restore the society to good ways.[7]

Interestingly, Caraka in his text, *Caraka Saṁhitā*, considers good values as *cikitsā* – he lays down the rules of conduct that help attain

> Seek and serve the good and avoid the bad human beings; be happy in the happiness of others; live a life of restraint and discipline *niyama*; do your duty without attachment; keep evenness of mind and intellect; control the "waves", cognitions, of the mind.

---

[6] It is another matter that modern Western literature is *afflictive* rather than restorative.

[7] *Nāṭyaśāstra* I.8-15.

These values are ingrained in the ordinary, average Indian mind and are very much a part of the lived life of people. He sums up these rules – *ṛte jñānam mukti*, there is no liberation (*mokṣa*) without knowledge. Right knowledge is the knowledge of right values and that knowledge liberates one from the suffering (*duḥkha*) here and now.

Caraka defines happy life as one with right values:

> A man with right values thinks of the well-being of others, considers others' wealth as *tuccha* (of no consequence) is possessed of acknowledged virtues, *sadguṇa* (such as truth-telling), acts thoughtfully, respects those who are worthy of respect, is indifferent (*udāsīna*) to others, serves, devotedly the learned and the aged, controls his passions, is constantly involved in sharing his knowledge, his wealth, sees all beings in his own self, accepts good advice.[8]

Ayurveda puts great value, generosity of spirit, kindness to others, respectful to elders, parents, teachers and guests, restraint in speech and movement, control over senses, absence of jealousy, worry, fear, possessed of humility, faith in God, devotion to those who excel in learning and arts, thoughtfulness and carefulness.

There is thus no opposition between "beauty" (aesthetics) and social/individual welfare (ethics) (a) in Indian art, including verbal art, and (b) in Indian theory of verbal art which includes in its domain both the *kavi* (poet) and the *śilpī* (craftsman). It is possible to show that *art* in India has always been wedded to knowledge (*jñāna*) and ethics (*puruṣārtha*). Examination of any one form of art – say narratives as verbal art – will show an evolution in the understanding of the goal of *all* art from promotion of personal ethics (*mokṣa*) to the establishment of public ethics (*lokasaṁgraha*), the movement

---

[8] *CS* 1.30.26

from the Upaniṣadic knowledge-narratives such as Naciketā to the Jātaka narratives of *bodhisattva*.

Saundarya, though it is the *property* that enables art to fulfil its *goal* (*lakṣaṇa* and *prayojana*), is not the defining property (locus, *ātmā*) of arts. Even as a property, it is not defined formally or in abstraction from the context of the artist, the object and the audience. Further, its nature (definition) is to be understood not only from theoretical discussions (by literary theorists in Kāvyaśāstra, for example) but also, and mainly from the practice of verbal art (and other arts) by not only poets but also philosophers. Even the potter's art is socially relevant and the *ghaṭa* (pitcher) he makes is a profound philosophical symbol (*ghaṭākāśa*) and also a very important element in the religious and social ritual and life of the Indian people.

Art restores good health of the individual and the society by imparting in a palatable manner the right values. We have the paradigm legend in Bharata's *Nāṭyaśāstra*:

> In the ancient days when people absorbed in desire and greed, adopted ways contrary to righteousness and were swayed by jealousy and anger and were victims of joy and sorrow, the *devatā*s appealed to Brahmā to create a means of entertainment fit for all classes and types of people. . . . Then Brahmā created *nāṭya*, the *pañcam veda* filled with serious philosophical ideas and knowledge of crafts to teach ordinary people appropriate *dharma* (principle of righteousness) and *artha* (valid material goals). . . . Then the text was taken from the *Ṛgveda*, music from *Sāmaveda*, enactment from *Yajurveda* and *rasa* (the aesthetic experience) from *Atharvaveda*.

Paraphrasing the legend one may say that arts have the status of "Veda", and like the Vedas, arts are also a means of achieving liberation from the suffering here and now. But Abhinavagupta, the eleventh-century Kāśmīrī philosopher and poetician, asks[9] how can art which is by definition *prapañcātmaka* (a construct of the mind) promote *lokācāra* (proper worldly conduct) or become the means of promoting the four ends of life and have the status of Veda? He himself explains that though this world itself is *asatya nāma-rūpa-prapañcātmaka* (a non-real name-form construct of the mind), through sensory cognitions and meditation (*manana*) on them it enables the realization of *puruṣārtha*s and by indicating the ultimate *puruṣārtha* that transcends this world, that of realizing the identification of the self with *Brahman* (the universal self) it becomes the means of establishing one in tranquillity (*śānta rasa*). So what the scholar of Veda achieves, the auditor of art also achieves. Through *rasa*s that are absorbed in the heart, one develops an intellect that leads him to *dharma* and frees him from *adharma*. So enjoining as it does, like the Vedas, what one must do and what one must not do with the advantage that its injunctions are like the medicine dissolved in milk, art is equated with Veda.

Thus from the beginning in India's intellectual traditions, art and ethics are deeply interwoven with each other.

---

9 For this and the ensuing discussion please see *Abhinavabhāratī* on *Nāṭyaśāstra* I, *kārikā*s 1, 4, 12, 14-16.

6

Characteristic Cultural Expressions, Sublime and Sṛṅgāra

Characteristic Cultural Expressions and Ages: Epic or Drama or Lyric or Prose

It is almost self-evident that cultures have given forms as their typical expressions. Thus India has epic as its characteristic expression, Greece has tragedy and England, lyric.

In the same way, different ages of a culture express themselves in different forms – Elizabethan age in lyrics, sixteenth and seventeenth-century England in drama, eighteenth century of England in prose and nineteenth in novel.

India's genius is epic and its characteristic expression is in *śravya–prekṣā* (aural–visual) compositions and the preferred form is "singable" poetry, both lyrical and narrative.

Sublime and Classic

Of late, in this so-called egalitarian age, all books are good and there are no "classics". This is a denial of the validity of evaluation of literary texts. But evaluation of poems and narratives has been a perennial pursuit. The parameter of excellence is some definition or other of "sublime" and what is sublime is acknowledged as a classic. Aristotle's discussion in *Poetics*, of what the poet is to aim at and what he is to avoid what are the conditions on which the tragic effect depends (section 13), what are the sources of fear and pity (section 14), what is the importance of moral purpose (section 15), what is the form of discovery (section 16) and his analysis of diction, particularly of the role of metaphor (section 22), are clearly the original impulses for Longinus' discussion of the sublime subject and sublime expression. Aristotle and Longinus are bridged by Horace's discussion of diction and by Demetrius (on style) who divides literary expression into "plain", "stately", "polished" and "powerful". Longinus' principle of sublimity, apart from being a descriptive category, is also an evaluative measure that can explain why "some works please all men at all times" (*On the Sublime*, chapter 7).

Several centuries later, Addison takes up this criterion of ". . . pleas(ing) all men at all times" in his essay *Chevy Chase*[1] and asserts that what pleases people of all times must be analysed for the properties that make it a "classic". If we follow this line of thinking, Homer who has been popular at all times and in all places and in translations into all languages is definitely a "classic" – and so are many others like him.

The rampant solipsism of the contemporary times has destabilized some fundamental milestones, reference points, of the human mind – perfection, excellence, goodness, beauty, selflessness, nobility, soul of man. But such "windy" times have happened often in human history and happen when many narratives compete with each other. Such times are "rich" in one sense in that many schools of thought take birth and they become so much diverse data, enabling the emergence and formulation of evaluative paradigms and judgements. Finally they need to have a new balance, a new standard and commonly agreed voices that evoke the past perfections and express new hopes. They become "re-activating" agents and that is how and why the masterpieces endure and have endured. Homer remains the great Homer and *Mahābhārata* remains a civlizational epic, solipsistic fears, regardless.

---

1 *The Spectator*, Nos. 70, 74: 1711.

Theories come and go, but some remain for ever because of their explanatory power and re-contextualizing potential. The questions are perennial as are some of the answers.

7

Theorizing Theory

A STUDENT of comparative literature may also feel the need to theorize about theory as part of his search for appropriate theory. Indian intellectuals, brought up as they are on "special" Western mental food, exclusively rely on Western, specifically, American, theories to understand the Indian reality. How far this exercise is valid or desirable needs to be thought about. Is a culturally alien theory "adequate" or a "good fit"? As all theory is culture specific, it is reasonable to argue that Indian literatures are best understood/explained by Indian theoretical frames. This is not an argument against the "universal" elements in all theory but theories vary according to how "local" they are, and the more "local" they are, more they are driven by specific, variable socio-intellectual conditions and more restricted is their applicability domain.

Therefore, there is need to theorize about theory/theories we use so that we may use the most appropriate theory, a good fit for the object we seek to understand/appreciate. This is a fundamental epistemological imperative.

Here we can only suggest the line of investigation. An examination along these lines will consider the following issues:

A

1. West as "theory" India as "data"

2. Indian academy and Western academy
3. Uncritical reception

B

1. Literature, criticism and theory – the three functions and relationship in talking about literature
2. Goal of literature in society and its status as rational discourse
3. Its use as a document in contemporary Western criticism
4. "Theory"

C

1. Cultural specificity of all theories – origin, history and nature
2. The "Indian" and the "Western" mind – foundationally different "drivers"

D

1. Contemporary literary theory – overview of origin, kinds, concerns
2. Its characteristic conflict-orientation
3. Do we need that in the Indian socio-intellectual/literary reality?

E

1. Is it "appropriate theory" for the essentially oral Indian literature/culture?
2. Indian poetics – its nature and character
3. Indian literary theories
4. Indian philosophy of literature

F

1. English departments and the research desiderata.

Most of these questions have been touched, even if marginally, in the present long essay – except perhaps "D" which has not been directly addressed or at least in much detail.

What is called simply "theory" now represents the post-1960s thinking about literature that marked a break from what is known as "liberal humanist" conception of literature and its elements, a thinking that originated during renaissance and is marked by great confidence in the abstract categories of essentially Christian thought wedded to the new concern for the welfare and comfort of man, the individual. Liberal humanist faith in the "essence" of everything, the availability of one "truth", unchanging givens, individuality and knowability of all this was subjected to three radical intellectual onslaughts: (i) the onslaught of Marxist questioning of the individual-centred thought and the non-evolutionary postulation of "unchanging" realities; (ii) the onslaught of Quantum Physics undermining "certainties", and (iii) the onslaught of the Saussurean linguistic turn that turned upside down and replaced the comfortable representational view of language by the constructivist view that reduced all "reality" to relativistic flux constructed by each individual consciousness.

With all certainty gone, the text became open with no fixed meaning and became vulnerable to all kinds of interpretation, a virtual anarchy of meaning. All approaches in the rubric of "theory" are proposals about the source and the nature of literary meaning. Is the source of meaning god or society or the author's mind or the reader's mind or socially constructed language, total discourse, the unconscious (of the author/reader), unintended, or just a by-product? Is the meaning moral/theological or social or political or of subjective experience or of subjective reading or psychological or discursive or random?

Major contemporary Western schools and theories are all marked by their recourse to linguistic exegesis, the almost exclusive reliance on language as the instrument of interpretation. This is true of Russian Formalists with their search for the characteristic literariness of literature, their concept of literature as an autonomous discipline and their research into narrative, stylistic, rhythmic and sound structures as well as the relationship between life and literature. It is also true of the morphologists with their research into types or genres and forms of literary discourse of the new critics (and other Anglo-Saxon schools) with their conception of autonomy of a literary work and their linguistic methods of analyses of structuralism and its later developments including deconstruction and post-modernism which developed under the influence of ethnology and linguistics with its focus on rhetorical, narrative and textual structures. These and other modern developments such as psycholinguistics and gender studies have all been inspired and influenced by Ferdinand de Saussure's "phonocentric revolution" in European thought what is also called the 'linguistic term'.

In its essentially linguistic character, contemporary literary thought shows interesting affinities with classical Indian literary theories and practices. It is not unreasonable to suppose, in view of the academic history of Europe,[1]

---

[1] We had noted in "Loss, Recovery and Renewal of Texts in Indian Traditions" (in *Evam: Forum on Indian Representations*, 3:1&2 (2004)): "All the major European minds of the nineteenth century – Humboldt, Fichte, Hegel, Goethe, Schopenhauer, Kant, Nietzsche, Schiller, Schelling, de Saussure, Roman Jakobson, Trubetzkoy, were either Sanskritists or, on their own admission, had been deeply involved in Indian thought. Their work has inspired various thought movements – Idealism, Romanticism – which have shaped the contemporary mind. For example, structuralism which owes so much to the work of de Saussure who was Professor of Sanskrit at Geneva before he came over to Sorbonne, is the underpinning of what are today virtually global thought-movements right up to and including Post-Modernism."

particularly Germany, that these affinities are not accidental or random but a systematic reflex of the study and research in Sanskrit philosophy, linguistics and literary theory in the eighteenth and nineteenth centuries. The "critical" theory of aesthetics propounded by Immanuel Kant (1724–1804) with its focus on the knowability of "phenomena" alone and the theory of aesthetic expression, and reception, of the singular in sensory images through a process of logical reasoning propounded by Croce (1866–1952) invite comparison with what Todorov had described as theories of "verbal symbolism" in the work of classical Sanskrit poeticians, Ānandavardhana and Abhinavagupta, and these are just two major instances of theoretical fusion in the two cultural traditions.

However, the character of "theory" has two defining properties that render it inappropriate for Indian literary situation – (i) these are ethnographic in their drive and therefore divisive in the way they foreground "identity" as a primary imperative, and, partly for this reason, (ii) in their genesis they are conflict-oriented. In an earlier study,[2] we extrapolated on the philosophy of knowledge in the West, the intellectual inheritor of the Hebraic tradition, contradictions with other Hebraic systems, Judaism and Islam, nonetheless. It is significant that in the Western tradition, "knowledge" has been opposed to innocence, is associated with "power" and leads to the fall of man. The renaissance must be seen as a watershed in the Western history of ideas when the ontological shift from God to man/nature and the epistemological shift from verbal authority and experience to reason and experiment marked the transition from the middle ages to the modern period. What is, however, common throughout the Western history of ideas is the man-centred

---

[2] See, *Knowledge, Individual and Society in Indian Traditions.* Chandigarh: Saini Memorial Foundation Lecture, Punjab University, 2002.

world-view. In the middle ages, God is the object of study for the sake of man, for his redemption. Renaissance onwards, focus shifts to nature as the object of study for the sake of man, for his comfort. It is interesting that a marked adversarial axis has always obtained between the Western man and his object of study. It is almost as if man is always threatened by, or is at the least in the presence of, an adversary who has to be subdued or neutralized or used in the interest of man. While through the middle ages, God entered into this adversarial relationship with man – seeking obedience from him, punishing him,[3] now nature becomes the great adversary and the new knowledge. Science is put to service to bend nature to man's purpose. In the nineteenth century it is man or a class of men against man or a class of men in the Marxist class-war doctrine and now in the twentieth century it is woman against man. The Hebraic man-centred view that subordinates everything to man's comfort is the obvious foundation for this conflict model, which informs practically all the Western disciplinary codes – sociological, economic and political, and is at the heart of the Darwinian evolutionary thought as well.

Knowledge is an instrument of power in this conflict model, an instrument to handle the "adversary". In the Old Testament, we have already noted, man is given "dominion over the fish of the sea, and over the fowl of the air, and over the cattle, and over all the earth. . . ."[4] The Western man has been granted this dominion and has treated it as a matter of his right to maintain and extend this dominion. Therefore, after renaissance, the whole project of knowledge is to bend nature to man's purpose, the purpose being to achieve a life of comfort, something that has been promised to him by his

[3] Old Testament, Deuteronomy, 4:10-43.

[4] Genesis 1:26.

God as a birthright. This explains the fruition of sciences into technology and the retreat of Christian ontology before the advancing empirical science which rendered much of Christian dogma indefensible and led finally to the collapse of faith with such drastic intellectual and spiritual consequences for the Western Christendom in the nineteenth century, the collapse of one of the legitimizing schemes that the post-modernists take note of.

Since renaissance, empirical sciences have enabled man to gain mastery over nature. But the ruthless exploitation and "bending" of nature has brought the mankind face to face with ecological disaster. The enlightenment project, seventeenth century onwards, explicitly put reason above faith in the pious expectation that the epistemological reordering would hasten the millennium, facilitate the second coming and establish a brave new world. The dream collapsed in the First World War trenches of Somme and Verdun and in the concentration camps such as Auschwitz and the carpet-bombing of German cities such as Dresden in the Second World War.

"Knowledge" in this paradigm is exteriorized and constituted in the empiricist mode through the senses and stored outside the mind in the "texts" that have or acquire societal authority. The individual is its passive recipient and user. Its power consists in the control it exercises over and the conformity it extracts from the individual and the "other" and as the Western history shows, this "organized" knowledge has often proved destructive. Its power rests in the authority of "truth" it attains through societal and institutional support. At a given time in the Western history, there has always been a dominant "truth" of the time. This is the consequence of the Hebraic-Semitic monistic imperative. Foucault points out that this imperative was "man" in the humanist phase. It is now "language" now. For Lyotard, it is "science" now. There is in the Western mind, a monistic imperative – a "truth" at a time. Between the dichotomies, only one is true and has to be cognized and then adhered to. This imperative is driven by the uncompromising monism of the Hebraic-Semitic world-view.[5]

And then why this search for certainty or definitiveness which has since been rejected by the contemporary Western thought? There was the assumption that there did exist a "definitive" truth, waiting to be grasped, of the objects and entities that constitute this world. In the Western threefold conception of language as a scriptal system as a representational (*not* constructivist),[6] a strong reality attached to the written word, which is graspable by visual perception. In all systems of thought visual perception is the strongest epistemology and one can see how one has to be careful not to psychically transfer the reality of the visual sign to what is denoted by the sign.[7] The reality of the object denoted is therefore taken for granted – what can be seen, exists – and language merely represents it.[8] But as we have already suggested above, following de Saussure, the West has

---

5 There is the argument now, the post-modernist argument that there is no one "truth" or "a truth" at all. This is ultimately an argument for plurality and/or nihilism for, in fact, the Vedāntic-Vaiyākaraṇa thought system.

6 Before Saussure's "phonocentric revolution" and before Derrida.

7 Bhartṛhari says in *Vākyapadīya* II that a wise man should examine carefully even the cognitions based in perception.

8 This conception of definitiveness or truth or reality of objects denoted by language is manifest in the Old Testament narrative of Moses returning from Mt. Sinai with the inscribed ten commandments and the implicit assumption of the reality of the transaction and of what was inscribed by the hand of God. Old Testament, Deuteronomy, 4:13: "And he declared ten commandments; and he wrote them up on two tablets of stone."

undergone "the linguistic turn" that led to a ontological shift – language is now seen as a constructivist system and a system of signs in which:

> The absence of the subject and the referent is a consequence of the possibility of signification in general, since the intelligibility of any sign whether spoken or written, depends on a differential network of signifiers . . . the deferral of the signified or "proper-meaning" is endless.[9]

So now we (= they) know that our knowledge by the fact of its being constituted in language is characteristically unstable. It is clear that the "contemporary" critique is quite in the "tradition" of Western history of ideas. There is distrust of knowledge (the "fall" syndrome) and knowledge is an exercise of power directed at certain ends (knowledge as an act) and as Aristotle had noted language connects "opinion" with categorical knowledge in that it makes "opinion" look like categorical knowledge. Certain kinds of knowledge, metaphysical for example, are constituted in the discourse and therefore may or may not express an absolute truth – this is the nature of verbal knowledge. All this is in the history of ideas.[10] Also the critique is chiefly concerned with the function

---

9 Joseph Adamson in *Encyclopedia*, op. cit., p. 297.

10 See, Bertrand Russell, particularly the following in his *Human Knowledge: Its Scope and Limits* (London: George Allen and Unwin, 1948):

Three ways of defining "knowledge" – self-evidence, coherence, beliefs that promote success. "Knowing is a matter of degree – highest in perception; next highest in mind memories."

"All knowledge is in some degree doubtful and we cannot say what degree of doubtfulness makes it cease to be knowledge, anymore than we can say how much loss of hair makes a man bald . . . since all knowledge (or almost all) is doubtful the concept 'uncertain knowledge' must be admitted." (pp. 516-17)

→

of knowledge, with how knowledge functions in the society (at the expense of the individual and his individuality). In this deconstruction is a political discourse in its assault on Christian metaphysical categories – after Marxism, yet another assault on Christianity, and as such it has definite theological ends as well.

In sum, the goal of knowledge is the gaining and exercise of "power". Its consequence is not always happy – in more fundamental terms, it leads to fall, which is tantamount to loss of freedom. Its categories (particularly metaphysical) are linguistic constructs but they are assigned "value"/"truth" through "legitimation" which in the case of such categories does not/cannot come from experience but comes instead from, outside itself and outside the individual who "knows". Such legitimation comes from some major belief system, a

---

→ "I do not wish to exaggerate the scope of pre-linguistic belief, only very simple and primitive matters can be dealt within the absence of words. Words are public, permanent (when written), and capable of being created at will . . . what is more, knowledge can be externalized in books of reference, and need then only exist in human beings when it is wanted" (p. 117). Marx: "The truth, i.e. reality and power, of thought must be demonstrated in practice." Russell says it applies to knowledge of general connections between sets. Leibniz's theory of knowledge, on the other hand "mirroring" the world applies to knowledge of facts – it is not demonstrable in practice" (p. 439). Russell goes on to say both views are insufficient: "sensation, perception, and memory are pre-verbal experiences . . . not different in animals from what they are in ourselves . . . when we come to knowledge expressed in words, we seem inevitably to lose something of the particularity of the experience that we seek to describe . . ." (p. 441).

Russell's concept of language as manifest audible verbalization is no longer acceptable as valid and is in any case at variance with the Indian theory of language as finally formulated by Bhartṛhari in his *Vākyapadīya* (I.17-20). However his position on the nature of knowledge is very close to the current thinking.

master narrative; say religion or science or aesthetics or ethics. In this structure, the individual has neither any role nor freedom (to evaluate for himself the validity of these categories of thought) as he is subjected to the societally exercised imposition of "belief".[11]

Therefore it is natural to raise questions about the appropriateness of monotheistic/monistic theoretical frameworks for what has always been a pluralistic and pluri-theistic society that is India. A culture that has, over thousands of years, welded together diverse ethnically different people speaking different languages and having different belief systems into a cultural and knowledge unity through synthesizing, transcendental frameworks of thought, cannot operate with divisive, ethnographic, conflict-oriented theories without damaging its harmonious unity. In India, traditionally *bheda buddhi* (difference-focusing intellect) is considered inferior and India has set up, as its intellectual goal, synthesis and harmony. The movement from *bheda* (difference) to *abheda* (non-difference) cannot accept divisive identity formation based in difference.

Hence, the need to theorize about theory.

—-*iti*—-

---

11 See, *Concept and Taxonomy of Knowledge* in the series History of Science, Culture and Civilization, D.P. Chattopadhyaya, General Editor, in the volume ed. G.C. Pande [under publication].

Bibliography

Western

Abercrombie, Lascelles, "A Plea for the Liberty of Interpreting" (1930), in *Selected Modern English Essays, Second Series*, London: Oxford University Press, 1932, pp. 202-31.

Addison, Joseph, *The Spectator*, ed. G.A. Smith (8 vols., London, 1897-98; E.L. 1907); ed. D.F. Bond (5 vols., 1965).

Aristotle, *On the Art of Poetry* (*Poetics*), tr. Ingram Bywater with a Preface by Gilbert Murray, Oxford Clarendon Press, 1920 (rpt. 1967).

Arnold, Matthew, *Essays in Criticism. Second Series*, ed. S.L. Littlewood, London: Macmillan, 1956.

Atkins, J.W.H., *English Literary Criticism*, 3 vols., Cambridge (later London), 1943-51.

Bacon, Francis, *Essays and Advancement of Learning*, The World's Classics 1937.

Coleridge, S.T., *Biographia Literaria*.

Daniel, Samuel, *Poems and a Defence of Ryme*, ed. A.C. Sprague Cambridge, Mass, 1930.

Demetrius, *On Style in Poetics and On Style and other Classical Writings on Criticism*, Everyman Library, 1935 (repr. 1949).

Dennis, John, *The Advancement and Reformation of Modern Poetry in English Critical Essays*, selected and ed. Edmund D. Jones, The World's Classics 1922, London: Oxford University Press (repr. 1961).

Dio Chrysostomus, "Philocetetes in the Tragedians", in *Classical Literary Criticism*, ed. D.A. Russell and M. Winter Bottom, Oxford, 1989.

Dryden, John, *Of Dramatic Poetry and Other Critical Essays*, ed. G. Watson, 2 vols., Everyman Library 1962, ed. Thomas Arnold Oxford: The Clarendon Press.

Eliot, T.S., *What Is a Classic?*, Faber and Faber, 1945.

—, *The Frontiers of Criticism*, The University of Minnesota, 1956.

— (ed.), *Selected Prose*, John Hayward Penguin, 1953.

—, *Essays Literary and Critical*, London: J.M. Dant, 1906 (repr. 1956).

Greene, D.J. (ed.), *Samuel Johnson: A Collection of Critical Essays*, Englewood Cliffs, 1965.

Hill, J.S., *Imagination in Coleridge* (annotated selections), London, 1978.

Horace, "The Art of Poetry", in *The Complete Works of Horace*, tr. Various Hands, London: J.M. Dent & Sons.

Johnson, Samuel, *Lives of the English Poets*, vol. 2, The World's Classics, 1905.

Jonson, Ben, *Timber, or Discoveries*, ed. G.B. Harrison, London, 1923.

Coburn, K. (ed.), *Coleridge: A Collection of Critical Essays*, N.J. Englewood Cliffs, 1967.

Leavis, F.R. *The Great Tradition*, London: Chatto & Windus, 1948.

—, *Revaluations, Penguin*, 1964.

—, *The Common Pursuit*, Pelican, 1962.

Longinus, "On the Sublime" in *Classical Literary Criticism*, Penguin.

Milton, John, "Preface to Samson Agonistes", in *Poetical Works*, ed. H. Darbishire.

Pater, Walter, *Appreciations* (1889), London: Macmillan, 1944.

Plato, *Dialogues*, tr. B. Jowett 3rd edn. 1892, repr. 1925.

Plotinus, *The Works*, tr. Stephen Mackenna London: Faber and Faber, 1917-30.

Plutarch, *Parallel Lives*, tr. Dryden, Everyman Library, *Selected Essays*, 2 vols., Oxford Translation Series.

Pope, Alexander "An Essay on Criticism" (1711), in *English Critical Essays, Sixteenth, Seventeenth and Eighteenth Centuries*, ed. Edmund D. Jones, The World's Classics, 1922 (repr. 1961).

Saintsbury, George, *A History of English Criticism*, Edinburgh, 1911.

Seiler, R.M. (ed.), *Walter Pater: The Critical Heritage*, London, 1980.

Shelley, "A Defence of Poetry", in Sidney, *An Apology for Poetry* and Shelley, *A Defence of Poetry*, ed. H.A. Needham, London: 1931 (repr. 1948).

Sidney, "An Apology for Poetry", in Sidney, *An Apology for Poetry* and Shelley, *A Defence of Poetry*, ed. H.A. Needham, London: 1931 (repr. 1948).

Augustine, St., *Confessions* (Translations of the *Confessions* and *De Civitate Dei* are contained in Everyman's Library).

Thomas Aquinas, St. Etienne Gilson, *The Philosophy of St. Thomas Aquinas*, tr. Edward Bullough, London, 1937.

Tacitus, Cornelius, "Dialogue on Orators", in D.A. Russell and M. Winter Bottom (eds.) *Classical Literary Criticism, Essays on Philosophy, Politics and Morals*, Oxford, 1989.

The World's Classics, 1905 (also in Everyman Library)

Trilling, Lionel, *Matthew Arnold* (rev. 3rd edn.), New York, 1963.

Vickers, B.W. (ed.), *Essential Articles on Francis Bacon*, London, 1972.

Ward, A.C. (selected and introduced), *Twelfth Night at the Old Vic*, 1933 (from *The Death of the Moth*, 1943) in *Specimens of English Dramatic Criticism XVII -XX Centuries*, London: Oxford University Press, 1945.

Watson, George, *The Literary Critics*, Penguin, 1962.

Wellek, Rene and Austin Warren, *Theory of Literature*, 1949, Penguin (Peregerine Books), Reissued 1985.

Wellek, Rene, *History of Modern Criticism*, 4 vols., New Haven, 1955.

Wimsatt Jr., W.K. and Cleanth Brooks, *Literary Criticism: A Short History*, New York, 1957.

Woolf, Virginia, "Modern Fiction" (from *The Common Reader*, J925) in *English Critical Essays, Twentieth Century*, selected and introduced) Phyllis M. Jones, London: Oxford University Press, 1954, pp. 388-99.

Wordsworth, William, *The Lyrical Ballads*, London: Methuen and Co., 1903 (repr. 1956).

Young, Edward, "Conjectures on Original Composition" (1759), in *English Critical Essays: Sixteenth, Seventeenth and Eighteenth Centuries*, The World's Classics, 1961.

Indian

Abhinavagupta, *Abhinavabhāratī* [for English translation of the exposition of *Rasasūtra*, see Gnoli; for Hindi translation of the complete work, see Vishveshvar].

—, *Locana* [for English translation, see Krishnamoorthy (1988)].

Ādi Śakarācārya, *Vivekacūḍāmaṇi* [for Hindi translation, see Munilal].

Agarwala, V.S., 1963a, *India as Known to Panini*, Lucknow: University of Lucknow.

—, 1963b, *The Thousand Syllabled Speech*, Varanasi: Published by author.

Aitareyopaniṣad [for English translation, see Swami Sarvananda (1955)].

Amarsingh, *Amarkośa* [for Hindi translation, see Sastri, Hargovinda].

Ānandavardhana, *Dhvanyāloka* [for English translation, see Krishnamoorthy (1981)].

Annamabhaṭṭa, *Tarkasaṁgraha* [for Hindi translation, see Sukla, Sricandradhara].

Ballantyne, J.K. and P.K. Mishra (tr.), 1967, *Sāhitya Darpaṇa*, Delhi: Motilal Banarsidass.

Belvalkar, S.K. (tr.), 1924, *Kāvyādarśa*, Poona: Oriental Book Agency.

Bhandarkar, R.G., 1883, "Development of Language and of Sanskrit", *Journal of the Bombay Branch of the Royal Asiatic Society*, **16**: 245-74.

Bhattacharya, Bishnupada, 1956, Constitution of Words: Sphota Theory and Its Opponents", *Our Heritage*, **4**: 217-26.

—, 1957, "Connotation of Words: A Comparative Study of the Viewpoints of Grammarians, Mimamsakas, and Naiyayikas", *Our Heritage*, **5**: 147-67.

—, 1958, *Yaska's Nirukta and the Science of Etymology: An Historical and Critical Survey*, Calcutta: K.L. Mukhopadhyaya.

—, 1962, *A Study in Language and Meaning: A Critical Examination of Some Aspects of Indian Semantics*, Calcutta: Progressive Publishers.

Bhattacharya, Ram Shankar, 1955, "Kinds of Exposition in Sanskrit Literature", *Annals of Bhandarkar Oriental Research Institute*, **36**: 123-32.

Bhattacharya, Shashthi Prasad, 1976, *Santa Rasa and Its Scope in Literature*, Calcutta: Sanskrit College.

Chaitanya, Krishna, 1965, *Sanskrit Poetics: A Critical and Comparative Study*, Bombay: Asia Publishing House.

—, 1983, *Cultural Leaders of India: Aesthetics*, New Delhi: Publications Division, Govt. of India.

Chakrabarti, Tarapada, 1971, *Indian Aesthetics and the Science of Language*, Calcutta: Sanskrit Pustak Bhandar.

Chari, V.K., 1992, *Sanskrit Criticism*, Delhi: Motilal Banarsidass.

Chatterjee, Haramba Nath, 1960, *Comparative Studies in Pali and Sanskrit Alamkaras*, Calcutta: Sanskrit Pustak Bhandar.

Chatterji, Kshitish Chandra, 1933, "Panini as Poet", *Calcutta Oriental Journal*, **1**: 47-56.

Coomaraswamy, Ananda K., 1957, *The Dance of Shiva*, New York: The Noonday Press.

—, 1981, *Figures of Speech or Figures of Thought*, Delhi: Munshiram Manoharlal.

Cowell, E.B. and A.E. Gough (tr.), 1981, *Sarvadarsanasamgraha*, ed. K.L. Joshi, Ahmedabad: Parimal Publications.

Dasgupta, Surendranath, 1922-55, *A History of Indian Philosophy*, 5 vols., Cambridge: Cambridge University Press.

Dasgupta, S.K. and S.K. De, 1947, *History of Sanskrit Literature*, Calcutta: University of Calcutta.

De, S.K. 1925, *Studies in the History of Sanskrit Poetics*, London: Luzac Co.

—, 1925, "The Theory of Rasa in Sanskrit Poetics", in *Sir Asutosh Mookerji Silver Jubilee Volumes*, vol. 3, pt. 2, Calcutta.

—, 1960, *A History of Sanskrit Poetics*, Calcutta: University of Calcutta.

—, 1963, *Sanskrit Poetics as a Study of Aesthetics*, Berkeley: University of California Press.

Dhayagude, Suresh, 1981, *Western and Indian Poetics: A Comparative Study*, Poona: Bhandarkar Oriental Research Institute.

Dwivedi, R.C. (ed.), 1969, *Principles of Literary Criticism in Sanskrit*, Delhi: Motilal Banarsidass.

—, (tr.), 1970, *The Poetic Light: Kāvya Prakāśa of Mammaṭa*, Delhi: Motilal Banarsidass.

Dwivedi, Rewa Prasad (ed. and tr.), 1979, *Alaṁkārasarvasva of Śrī Rājānaka Ruyyaka and Maṅkha* (in Hindi), Varanasi: Chowkhamba Sanskrit Sansthan.

—, (ed. and tr.), 1982, *Vyaktiviveka of Rājānaka Śrī Mahimabhaṭṭa* (in Hindi), Varanasi: Chowkhamba Sanskrit Sansthan.

Edgerton, F., 1938, "Etymology and Interpretation", *Proceedings of the American Philosophical Society*, **78**(4): 705-15.

Gerow, Edwin, 1971, A Glossary of Indian Figures of Speech, The Hague: Mouton.

Ghosh, Manmohan (tr.), 1950, *Nāṭyaśāstra*, Calcutta: Asiatic Society.

Gnoli, Raniero (tr.), 1985, *The Aesthetic Experience According to Abhinavagupta*, Varanasi: Chowkhamba Sanskrit Series Office.

Gokak, V.K., 1968, *An Integral View of Poetry*, New Delhi: Abhinav Publications.

Greimas, Algirdas Julien, 1971, "Narrative Grammar: Units and Levels", *Modern Language Notes*, **86:** 793-806.

Heimann, Betty, 1937, *Indian and Western Philosophy: A Study in Contrasts*, London: George Allen and Unwin.

—, 1941, "Sphota and Artha", in *P.V. Kane Festschrift*, Poona: Oriental Book Agency.

Hiriyanna, M., 1954, *Art Experience*, Mysore: Kavyalaya Publishers,

Ivanov, Vyacheslav V., 1974, "Growth of the Theoretical Framework of Modern Poetics", in *Current Trends in Linguistics*, ed. T.A. Sebeok, vol. 12, The Hague: Mouton.

Jacob, G.A., 1925, *Laukikanyāyāñjali*, Part 2, A Second Handful of Popular Maxims, Bombay: Nirnaya Sagar Press.

Jha, Sir Ganganatha (tr.), 1925, *Kāvyaprākśa*, Allahabad: Indian Book House.

—, (tr.), 1928, *Kāvyālaṁkārasūtra*, Poona: Oriental Book Agency.

—, (tr.), 1933, *Śābara Bhāṣya*, 3 vols., Baroda: Oriental Institute.

—, (tr.) [1900-1908], 1983a, *Ślokavārttika*, Delhi: Sri Satguru Publications.

—, (tr.) [1903-24], 1983b, *Tantravārttika*, Delhi: Sri Satguru Publications.

Jha, Madanmohan (ed. and tr.), 1987, *Rasagaṅgādhara* (in Hindi), Varanasi: Chowkhamba Vidya Bhawan.

Kane, P.V., 1951a, *History of Sanskrit Poetics*, Delhi: Motilal Banarsidass.

— (ed. and tr.), 1951b, *Sāhitya-Darpaṇa*, Bombay: Nirnaya Sagar Press.

Kapoor, Kapil, 1985, "Metaphor in Sanskrit and English Criticism", *Journal of Literary Criticism*, **2**(2): 29-44.

—, 1989, "Alaṁkāra and the Theory of Metaphor", in *Sanskrit Poetics and Western Thought*, ed. M.S. Kushwaha, Lucknow: Argo.

—, 1990, "Interpretation of Texts in the Indian Tradition", in *Structures of Signification*, ed. H.S. Gill, vol. 1, New Delhi: Wiley Eastern.

——, 1991, "Bhartṛhari on Lexical Meaning", in *Linguistics at Large: S.K. Verma Festschrift*, ed. V. Prakasam, Hyderabad: Booklinks Corporation.

——, 1992, "Norm and Variation: Pāṇini to Kumārila Bhaṭṭa: A Classical Indian Debate", in *Language and Text: A. Kelkar Festschrift*, ed. R.N. Srivastava, Delhi: Kalinga Publishers.

——, 1992, "Oral Narrative and Tense: A Description", in *Aspect, Tense and Mood in Hindi*, ed. Chaturbhuja Sahay, Agra: Central Institute of Hindi.

——, 1994, *Language, Linguistics and Literature: The Indian Perspective*, Delhi: Academic Foundation.

——, 1994, "Vivakṣā and Tātparya: Bhartṛhari on Speaker's Perception and Intention", in *Linguistics and Linguistics*, ed. Srihari Rao, vol. 2, Raipur: Indian Scholar Publications.

——, 1995, *Canonical Texts of English Literary Criticism*, Delhi: Academic Foundation.

——, 1996, "Theory of the Novel: The Indian View", in *Indian Response to Critical Theory*, K. Kapoor and Ranga Kapoor (ed.), 1994, "Mahāvākya: The Indian Theory of Literary Discourse", in *Confederate Gestures: Search for Method in Indian Literature Studies*, ed. Charusheel Singh, New Delhi: Associated Publishing House.

——, 1998 *Literary Theory: Indian Conceptual Framework*, New Delhi: Afliated East–West Press.

——, 2011, *Rati–Bhakti: Bharat kī kathā paramparā meṅ*, New Delhi: D.K. Printworld.

Kaur, Amarjit, 1979, *Influence of Indian Philosophy on Sanskrit Poetics*, Delhi: Bharatiya Vidya Prakashan.

Keith, A.B., 1924, *The Sanskrit Drama*, Oxford: Clarendon Press.

Krishnamoorthy, K., 1964, *Essays in Sanskrit Criticism*, Dharwar: Karnataka University.

——, 1968, *Some Thoughts on Indian Aesthetics and Literary Criticism*, Mysore: University of Mysore.

——, (tr.), 1977, *Vakroktijīvita*, Dharwar: Karnataka University.

——, 1979, *Studies in Indian Aesthetics and Criticism*, Mysore: D.V.K. Moorthy.

——, (tr.), 1981, *Dhvanyaloka*, Delhi: Motilal Banarsidass.

——, 1985, *Indian Literary Theories*, Delhi: Meharchand Lachman Dass.

___ (tr.), 1988, *Locana*, Delhi: Meharchand Lachman Dass.

Kunjunni Raja, K., 1954, "The Theory of Meaning According to the Buddhist Logicians", *Adyar Library Bulletin,* **18**: 178-95.

——, 1955, "Indian Theories on Homophones and Homonyms", *Adyar Library Bulletin,* **19**: 193-222.

——, 1955, "The Theory of Suggestion in Indian Semantics", *Adyar Library Bulletin,* **19**: 20-26.

——, 1956, "Sphota: The Theory of Linguistic Symbols", *Adyar Library Bulletin,* **20**: 84-116.

——, 1956, "Transfer of Meaning: A Buddhist View", *Adyar Library Bulletin,* **20**: 345-48.

——, 1957, "Akanksa: The Main Basis of Syntactic Unity", *Adyar Library Bulletin,* **21**: 282-95.

1962, "Prarthayanti: A Ghost Word Discussed by the Grammarians", *Adyar Library Bulletin* **26**: 26-28.

——, 1963, *Indian Theories of Meaning,* Madras: Adyar Library.

——, 1964, *Bhartrhari's List of Sentence Definitions, Adyar Library Bulletin,* **28**: 206-10.

——, 1965, "Pāṇini's Attitude Towards Lakṣṇa", *Adyar Library Bulletin,* **29**: 177-87.

Kushwaha, M.S. (ed.), 1989, *Sanskrit Poetics and Western Thought,* Lucknow: Argo.

——, 1991, *New Perspectives on Indian Poetics,* Lucknow: Argo.

Lahiri, P.C., 1937, *Concept of Riti and Guna in Sanskrit Poetics,* Dacca: University of Dacca.

Matilal, B.K., 1985, *Logic, Language and Reality,* Delhi: Motilal Banarsidass.

Mohan, G.B., 1968, *The Response to Poetry: A Study in Comparative Aesthetics,* New Delhi: People's Publishing House.

Mookerji, Radha Kumud, 1923, "History of Sanskrit Literature from the Works of Panini, Katyayana and Patanjali", *Indian Antiquary,* **52**: 21-24.

Mookerji, S., 1935, *The Buddhist Philosophy of Universal Flux,* Delhi: Motilal Banarsidass.

Munilal (tr.), 1996, *Vivekacūḍāmaṇi* (in Hindi), Gorakhpur: Gita Press.

Nagar, Ravishankar and K.L. Joshi (eds. and trs.), 1984, *Nāṭyaśāstra* (in Hindi), Ahmedabad: Parimal Publications.

Pandey, K.C., 1959, *Indian Aesthetics,* Varanasi: Chowkhamba Sanskrit Series Office.

Parashar, Sadhana (tr.), 1993, "Kāvyamīmāṁsā", New Delhi: D.K. Printworld.

Pusalkar, A.D., 1962, "The Rāmāyaṇa: Its History and Character", in *Cultural Heritage of India*, vol. 2, ed. S.K. De, U. Ghoshal, A.D. Pusalkar and R.C. Hazra, Calcutta: Ramakrishna Mission Institute of Culture.

Radhakrishnan, S. (tr.), 1948, *Bhagavadgītā*, London: George Allen and Unvin.

—, (tr.) 1956, *The Ten Principal Upaniṣads*, London: George Allen and Unwin.

Raghavan, V., 1940, *The Number of Rasas*, Madras: Adyar Library.

—, 1942, *Studies on Some Concepts of Alankarasastra*, Madras: Adyar Library.

—, (tr.), 1963, *Bhoja's Śṛṅgāraprakāśa*, Madras: Punarvasu.

—, 1978, "Sanskrit Kavya Literature: A General Survey", in *Cultural Heritage of India*, vol. 5, ed. Suniti Kumar Chatterjee, Calcutta: Ramakrishna Mission Institute of Culture.

Raghavan, V. and Nagendra (eds.), 1970, *An Introduction to Indian Poetics*, New Delhi: Macmillan India.

Ramakrishna Mission Institute of Culture, 1958-86, *Cultural Heritage of India*, 6 vols., Calcutta.

Rayan, Krishna, 1977, *Suggestion and Statement in Poetry*, London: University of London.

—, 1987, *Text and Sub-text: Suggestion in Literature*, New Delhi: Arnold Heinemann.

___, 1988, *The Burning Bush: Suggestion in Indian Literature*, Delhi: B.R. Publishers.

—, 1991, *Sahitya: A Theory*, New Delhi: Sterling Publishers.

Sahay, Rajvansh ("Hira"), 1973, *Dictionary of Indian Poetics* (in Hindi), Patna: Bihar Granth Academy.

Sankaran, A., 1929, *The Theories of Rasa and Dhvani*, Madras: University of Madras.

—, 1973, *Some Aspects of Literary Criticism in Sanskrit*, Madras: University of Madras.

Sarasvat, Pt. Kedarnath Sharma (tr.), 1954, *Kāvyamīmāṁsā* (in Hindi), Patna: Bihar Rashtra Bhasa Parisad.

Sarup, L. (ed. and tr.), 1967, *Nirukta and Nighaṇṭu*, Delhi: Motilal Banarsidass.

Sastri, Gaurinath, 1959, *The Philosophy of Word and Meaning*, Calcutta: Sanskrit College.

—, 1978, "Sanskrit Poetics" in *Cultural Heritage of India*, vol. 5, ed. Suniti Kumar Chatterjee, Calcutta: Ramakrishna Mission Institute of Culture.

___, 1987, *History of Classical Sanskrit Literature*, Delhi: Motilal Banarsidass.

Sastri, Pt. Hargovinda (tr.), 1984, *Amarakośa* (in Hindi), Varanasi: Chowkhamba Sanskrit Series Office.

Sastri, V.A. Rarnaswami, 1942, *Jagannatha Pandita: A Study*, Annamalai: Annamalai University.

Sastry, P.U. Naganatha (ed. and tr.), 1970, *Kāvyālaṁkāra*, Delhi: Motilal Banarsidass.

Seturāman, V.S. (ed.), 1992, *Indian Aesthetics: An Introduction*, New Delhi: Macmillan India.

Shree Purohit Swami (tr.), 1917, *Aphorisms of Yoga by Bhagwan Shree Patanjali*, London: Faber and Faber.

Spinoza, B., (n.d.) "The Interpretation of Scriptures", *The Philosophy of Spinoza*, ed. Joseph Ratmer, New York: Carlton House.

Sriramamurti, P., 1978, *Discourse Analysis in Sanskrit*, Visakhapatnam: Matrividya.

—, 1985, "The Concept of Mahavakya According to Vaiyakaranas", in *Professor Kuppuswami Sastri Centenary Volume*, Pt. 2, Madras: Kuppuswami Sastri Research Institute.

Srivastava, R.N. and K. Kapoor, 1988, "Semiotics in India", in *The Semiotic Web 1987*, ed. T.A. Sebeok and Jean Umiker-Sebeok, The Hague: Mouton.

Stall, Johan Frederik, 1969, "Sanskrit Philosophy of Language", in *Current Trends in Linguistics*, ed. T.A. Sebeok, vol. 5, The Hague: Mouton.

Stcherbatsky, Th., 1962, *Buddhist Logic*, 2 vols., New York: Dover.

Subramania Iyer, K.A., 1935, "Who Are the Anitya Sphoṭavadinaḥ?" *Proceedings of the All India Oriental Conference*, Mysore.

—, 1941, "Pratibha as the Meaning of a Sentence", *Proceedings of the All India Oriental Conference*, Tirupati.

—, 1947, "The Doctrine of Sphota", *Journal of Ganganatha Jha Research Institute*, **2**: 121-47.

—, 1965, "Bhartrhari on Dhvani", *Annals of Baroda Oriental Research Institute*, **46**: 49-65.

—, (ed. and tr.), 1965, *The Vākyapadīya of Bhartṛhari with the Vṛtti*, chapter 1 of *Vākyapadīya*, Poona: Deccan College.

—, 1968, "Bhartrhari on the Primary and Secondary Meaning of Words", in *S.M. Katre Festschrift*, vol. 1, Poona: Deccan College.

—, (tr.), 1969, *Bhartṛhari: A Study of the Vākyapadīya in the Light of Ancient Commentaries*, Poona: Deccan College.

—, (ed. and tr.), 1971, *The Vākyapadīya of Bhartrhaṛi*, chapter 3, part 1 of *Vākyapadīya*, Poona: Deccan College.

—, (ed. and tr.) 1973, *The Vākyapadīya of Bhartṛhari with the Prakīrṇa Prakāśa of Helārāja*, chapter 3, part 2 of *Vākyapadīya*, Poona: Deccan College.

— (ed. and tr.), 1977, *The Vākyapadīya of Bhartṛhari*, chapter 2 of *Vākyapadīya*, Delhi: Motilal Banarsidass.

Subramanian, A.V., 1988, *Aesthetics of Wonder*, Delhi: Motilal Banarsidass.

Sukla, Acarya Rarnacandra, 1947, *Rasa Mīmāṁsā* (in Hindi), Varanasi: Nagari Pracarani Sabha.

Swami Sarvananda (ed. and tr.), 1955, *Aitareyopaniṣad*, Madras: Sri Ramakrishna Math.

— (tr.), 1958, *Taittiriyopaniṣad*, Madras: Sri Ramakrishna Math.

Swami Tyagisananda (ed. and tr.), 1964, *Śvetāśvataropaniṣad*, Madras: Sri Ramakrishna Math.

Swami Vireshwarananda (ed. and tr.), 1978, *Brahmasūtra*, Calcutta: Advaita Ashram.

Tiwary, R.S., 1984, *A Critical Approach to Classical Indian Poetics*, Varanasi: Chaukhambha Orientalia.

Todorov, Tzvetan, 1982, *Symbolism and Interpretation*, translated from the French by Catherine Porter, London: Routledge and Kegan Paul.

Vaidya, P.L. and A.D. Pusalkar, 1962, "The Mahabharata: Its History and Character", in *Cultural Heritage of India*, vol. 2, ed. S.K. De, U. Ghoshal, A.D. Pusalkar and R.C. Hazra, Calcutta: Ramakrishna Mission Institute of Culture.

Vasu, S.C. [1891] 1980, *Aṣṭādhyāyī*, 2 vols., Delhi: Motilal Banarsidass.

Vishveshvar, Acarya (ed. and tr.), 1965, *Hindi Abhinavabhāratī*, Delhi: University of Delhi.

Viswanatha, *Sāhitya Darpaṇa* [for English translations, see Ballantyne, J.K. and P.K. Mishra, and also P.V. Kane (1951b)].

Von Glasenapp, Helmuth, 1973, *Image of India*, translated from the German by S. Ambike, New Delhi: Indian Council for Cultural Relations.

Walimbe, Y.S., 1980, *Abhinavagupta on Indian Aesthetics*, Delhi: Ajanta Books International.

Warder, A.K., 1972, *Indian Kavya Literature*, vol. 1, Delhi: Motilal Banarsidass.

—, 1978, *The Science of Criticism in India*, Madras: Adyar Library and Research Centre.

Zimmer, H., 1952, *Philosophies of India*, London: Kegan Paul.

Index